40 Outfits To Style

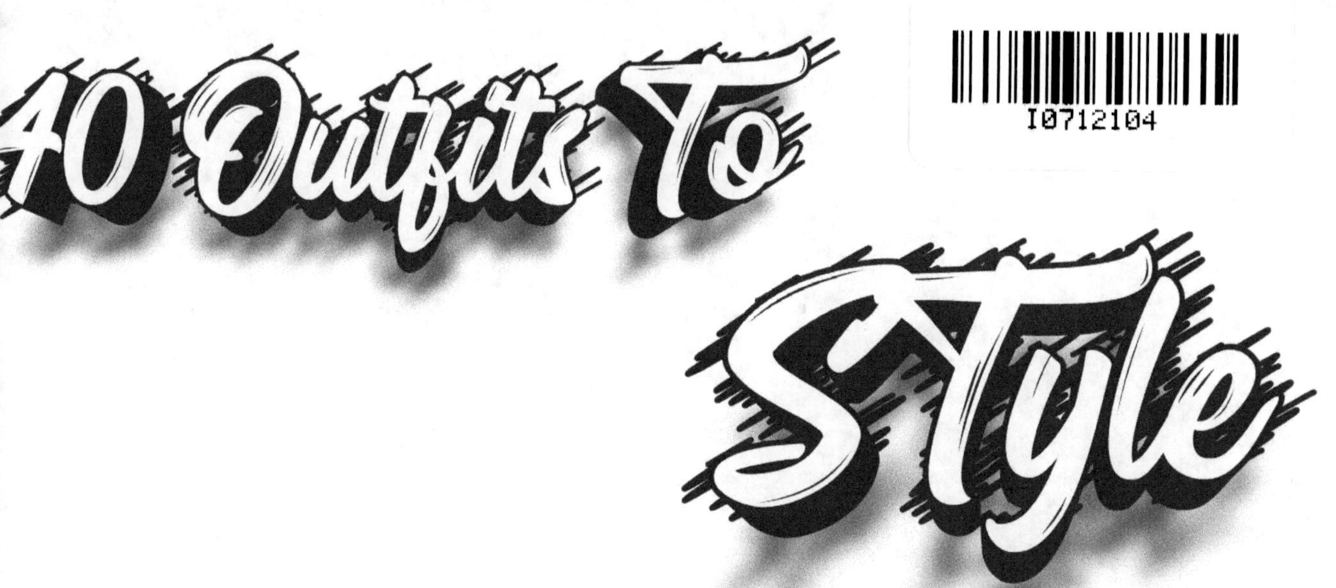

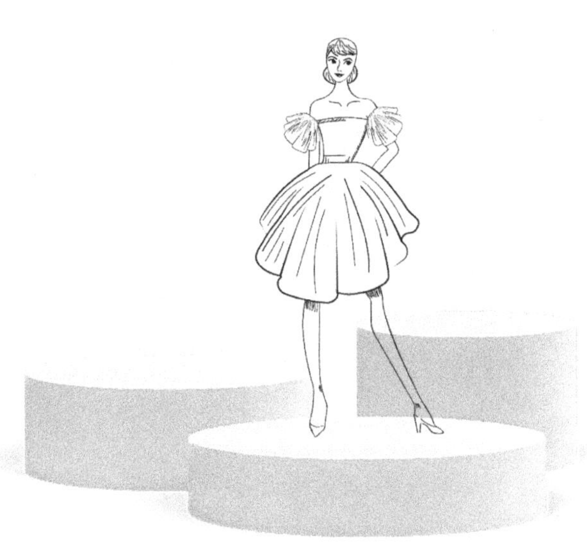

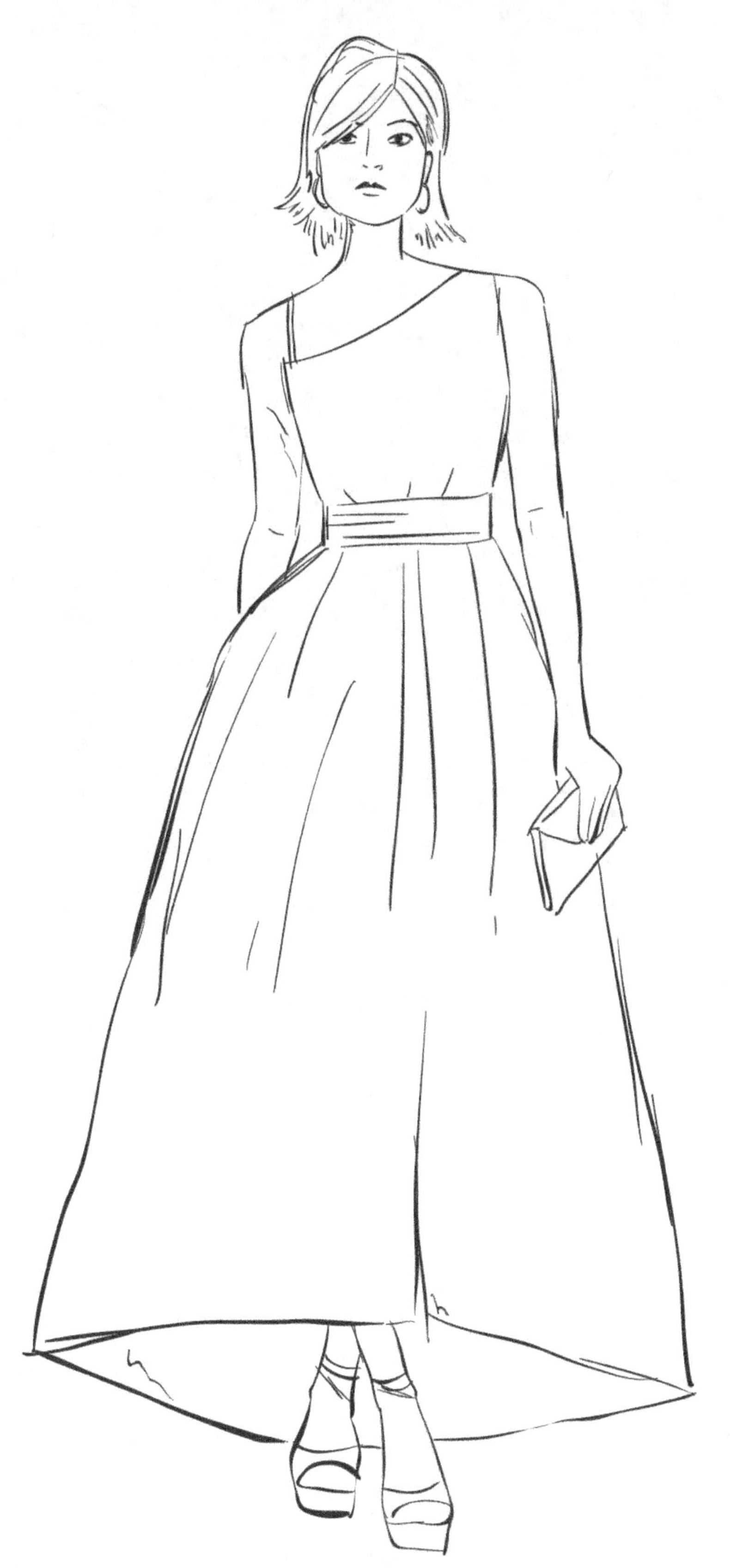

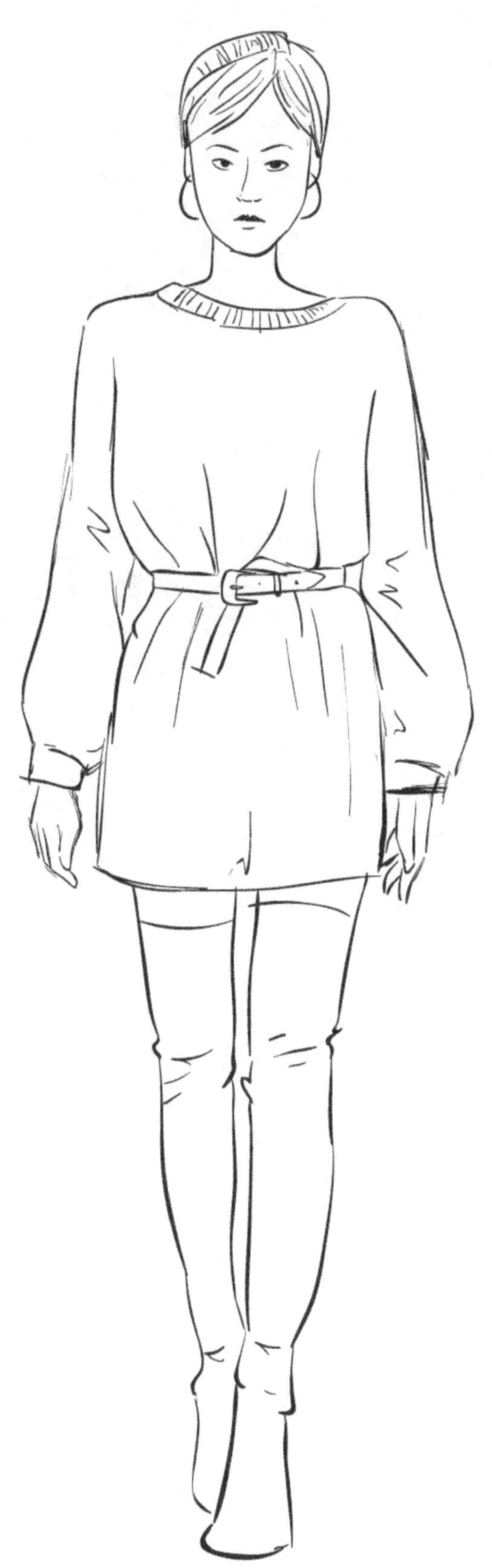

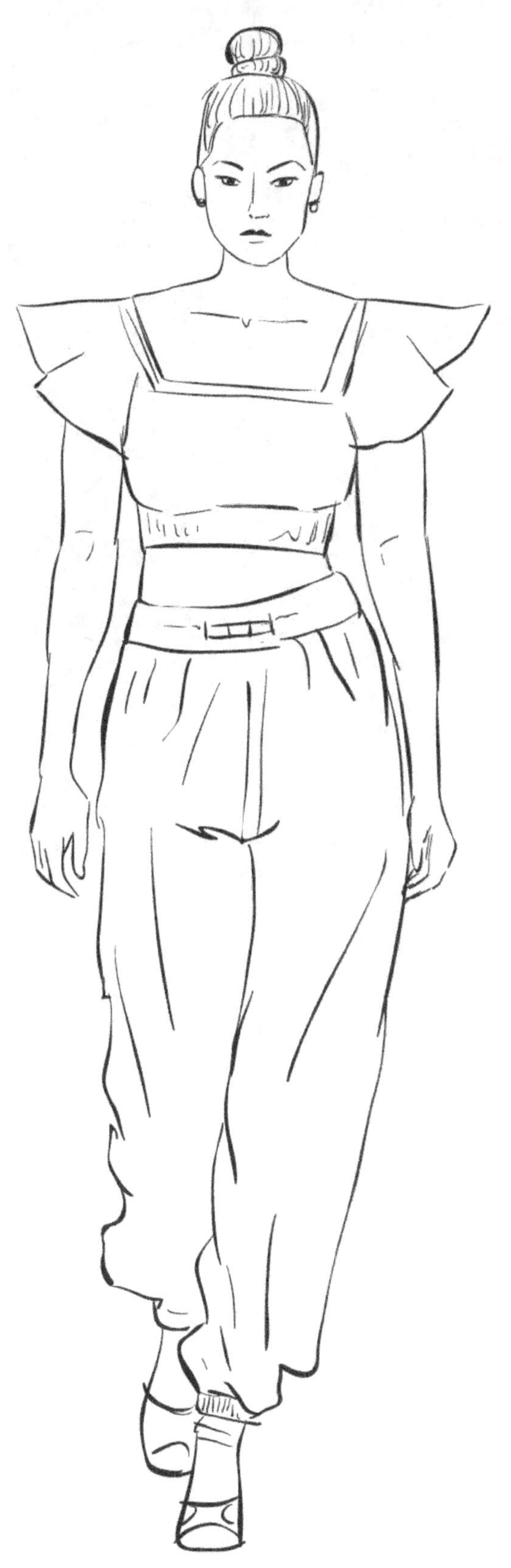

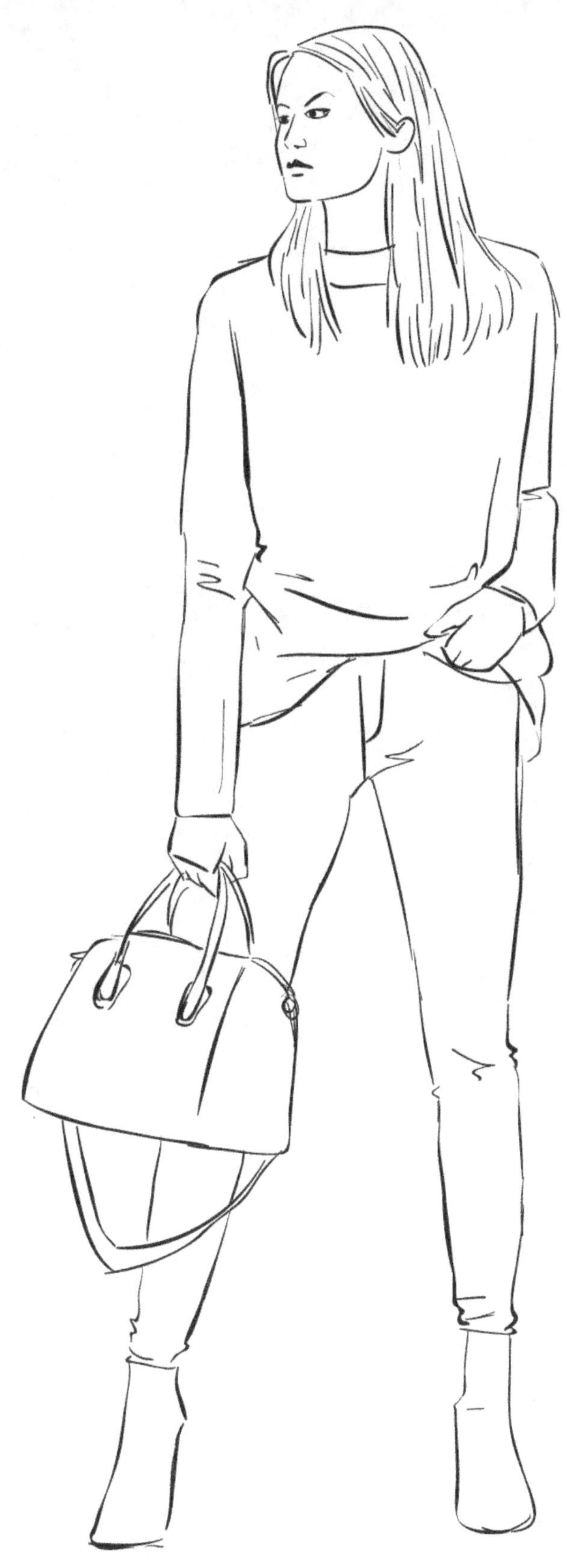

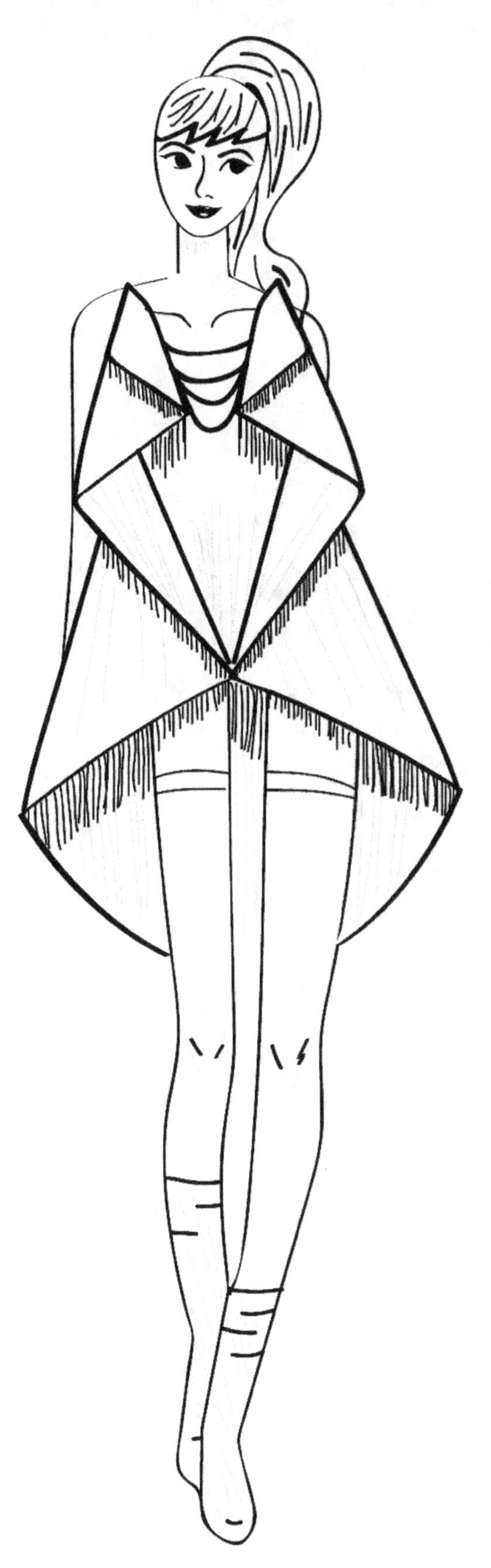

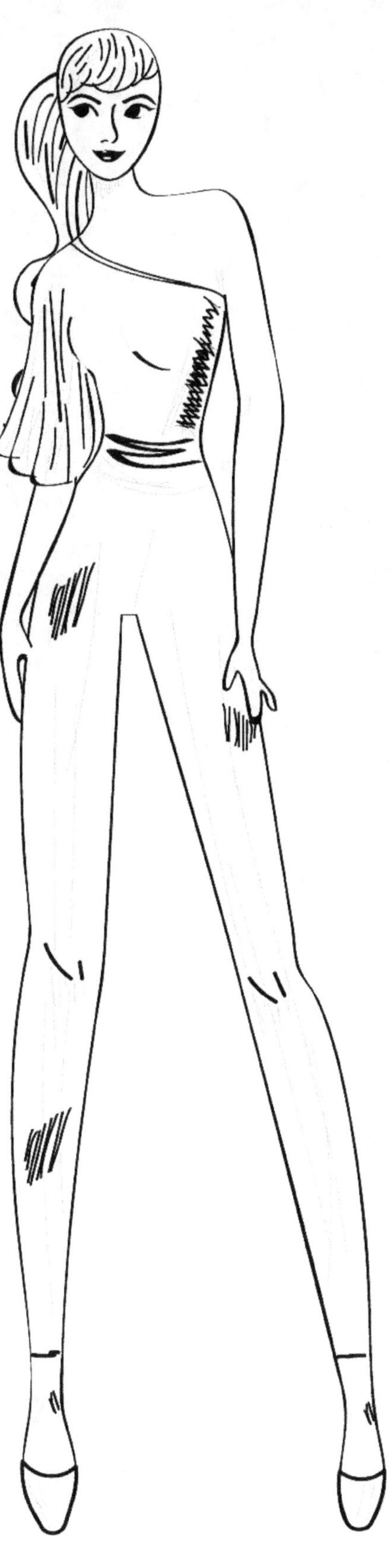

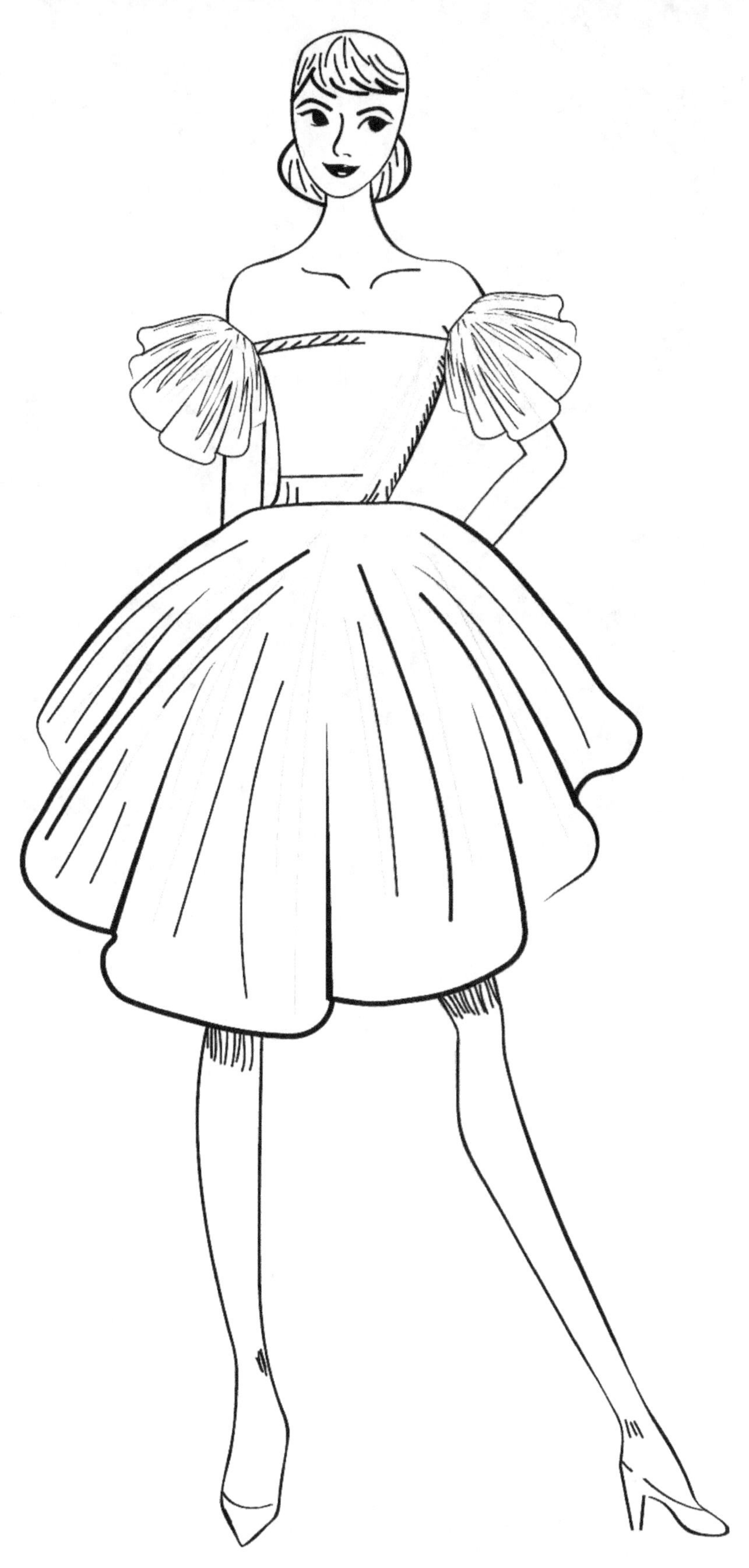

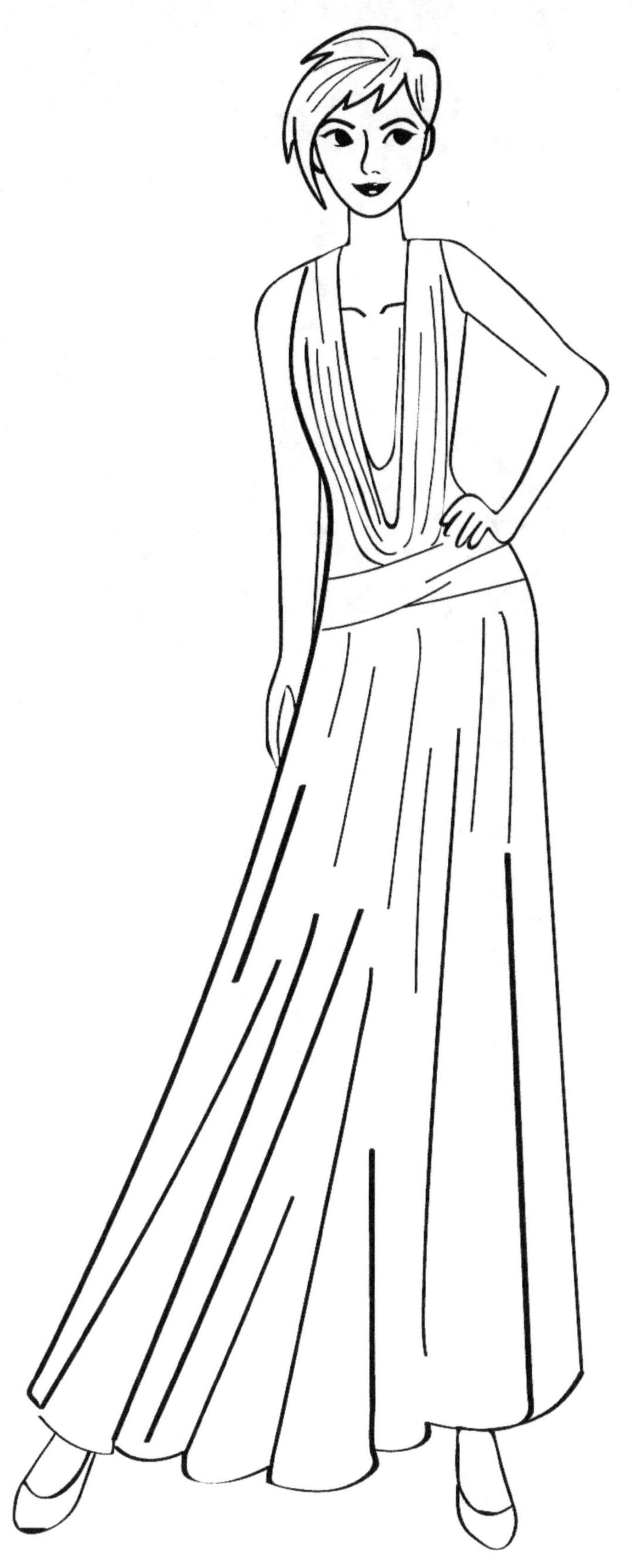

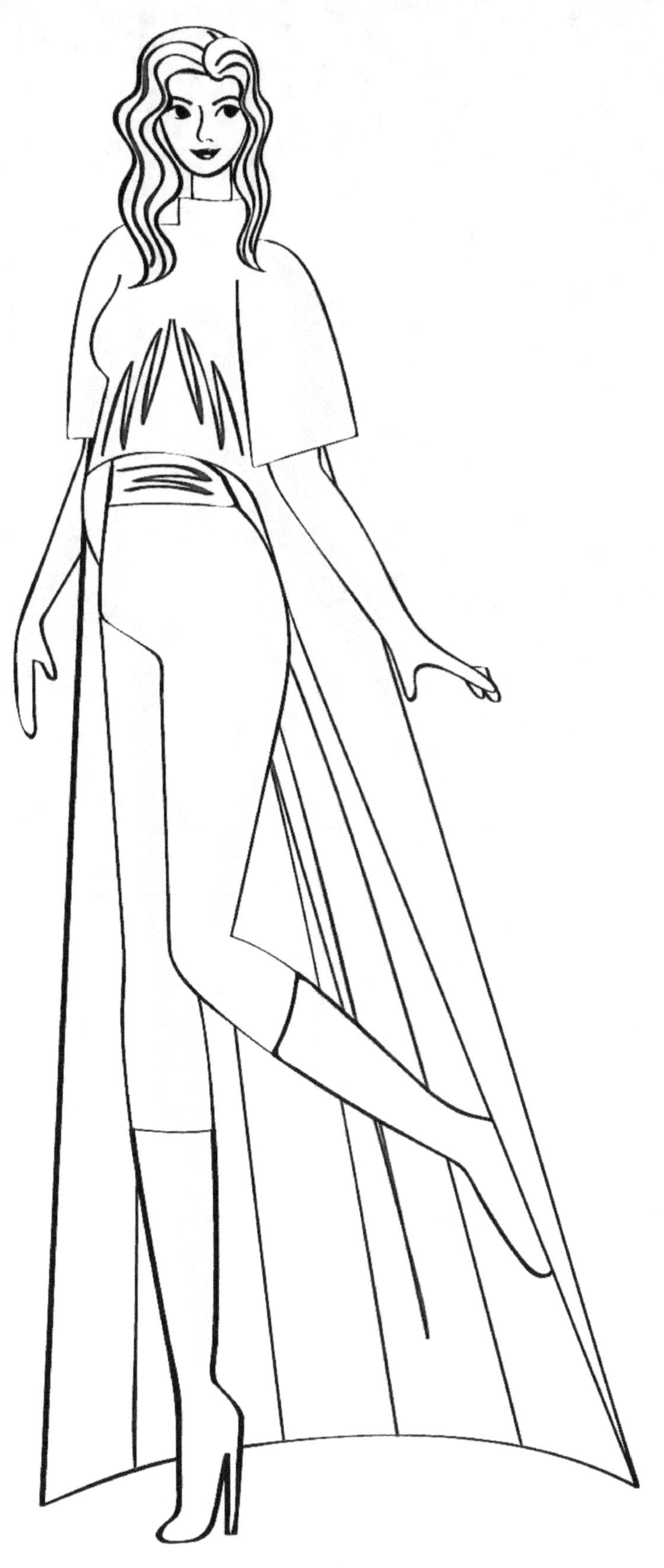

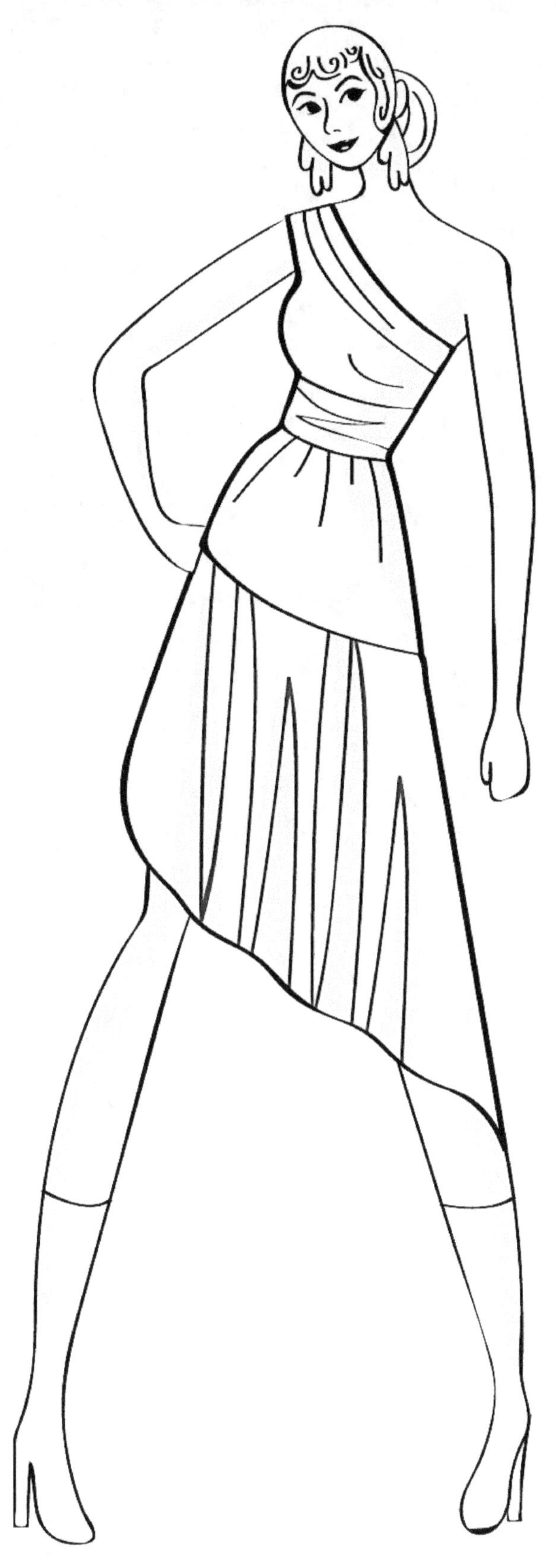

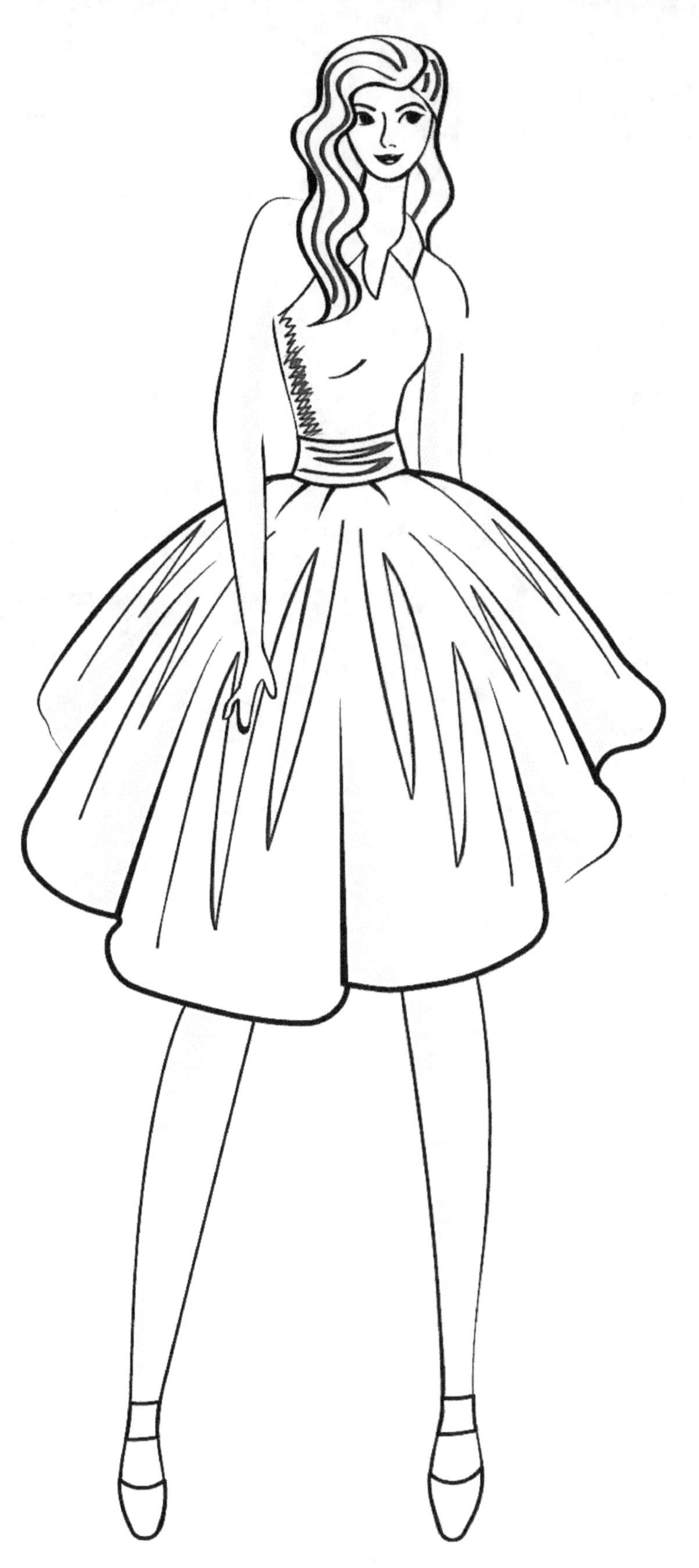

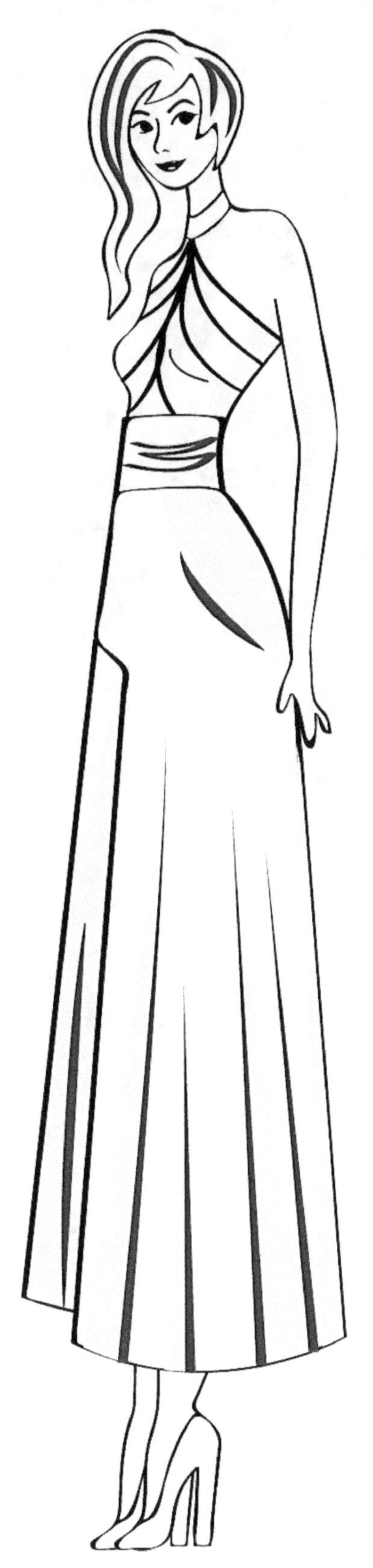

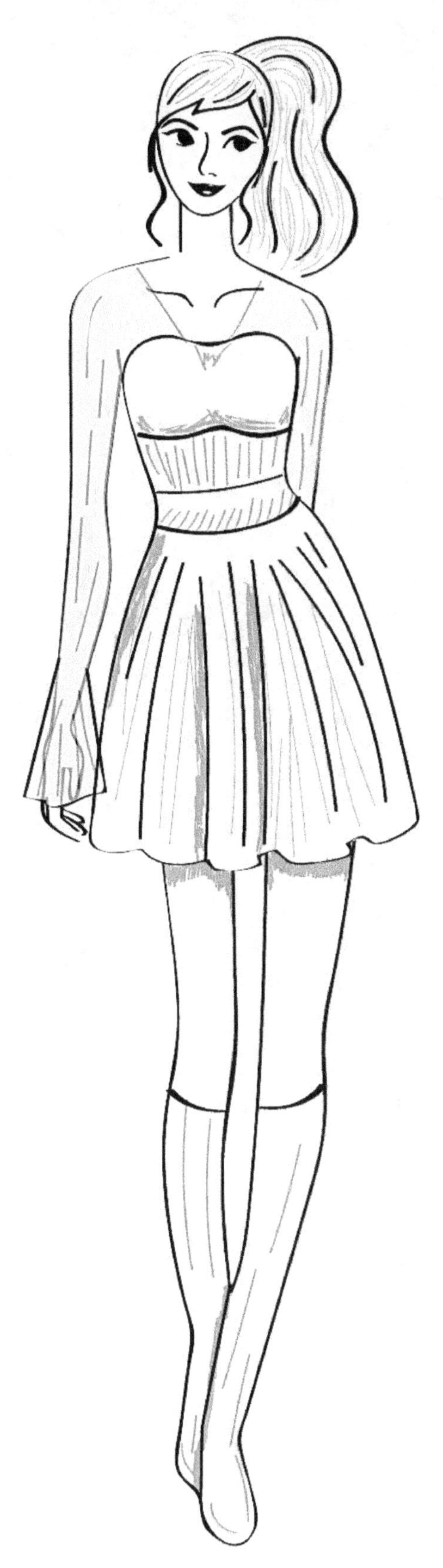

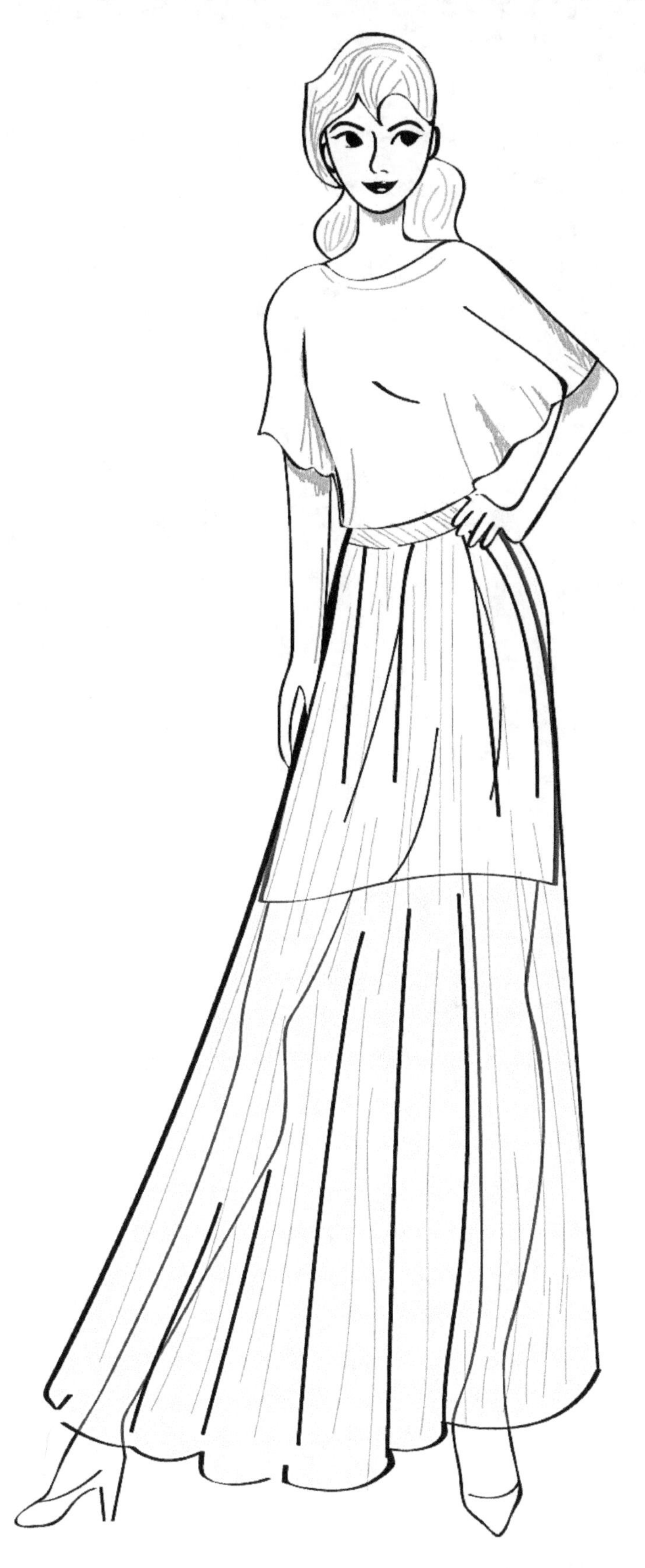

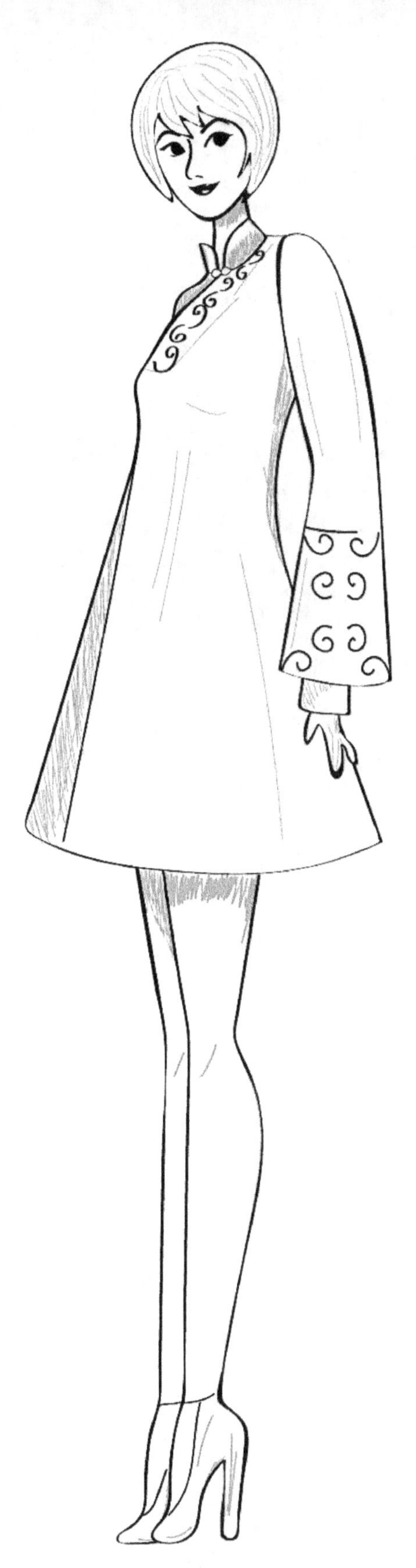

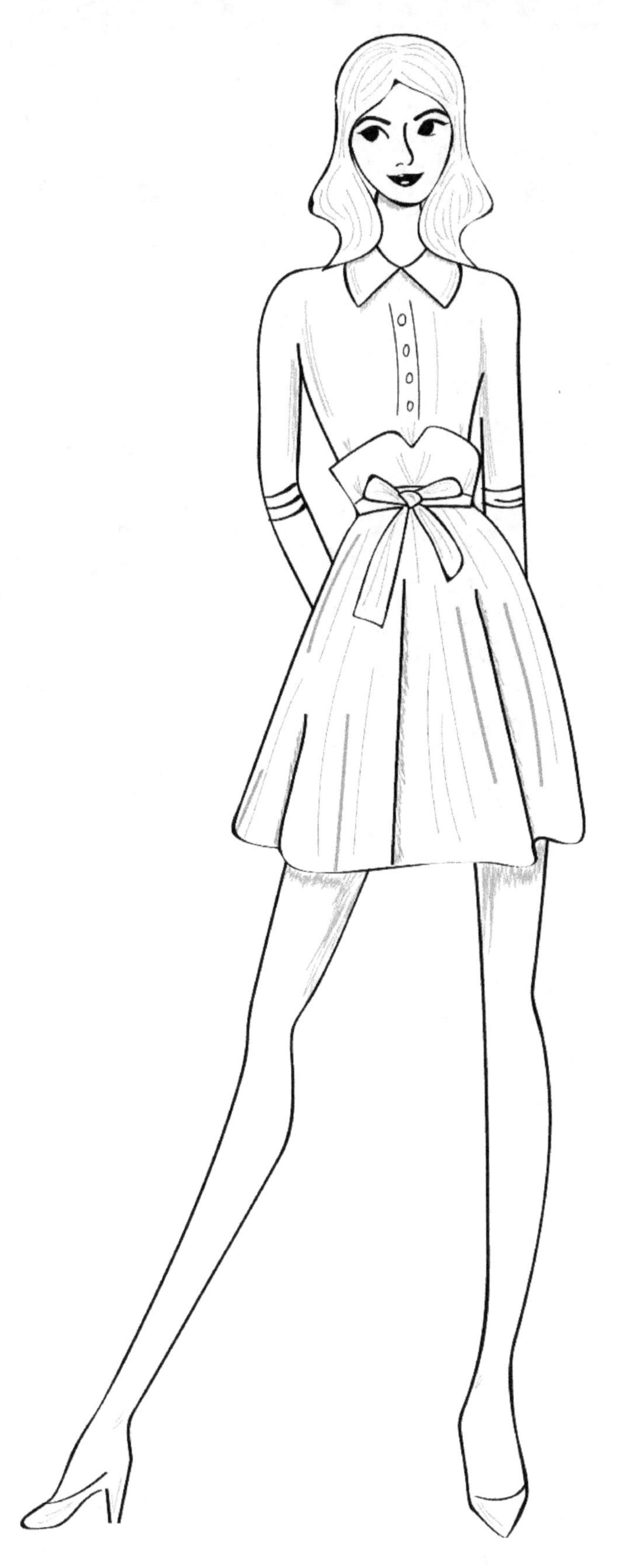

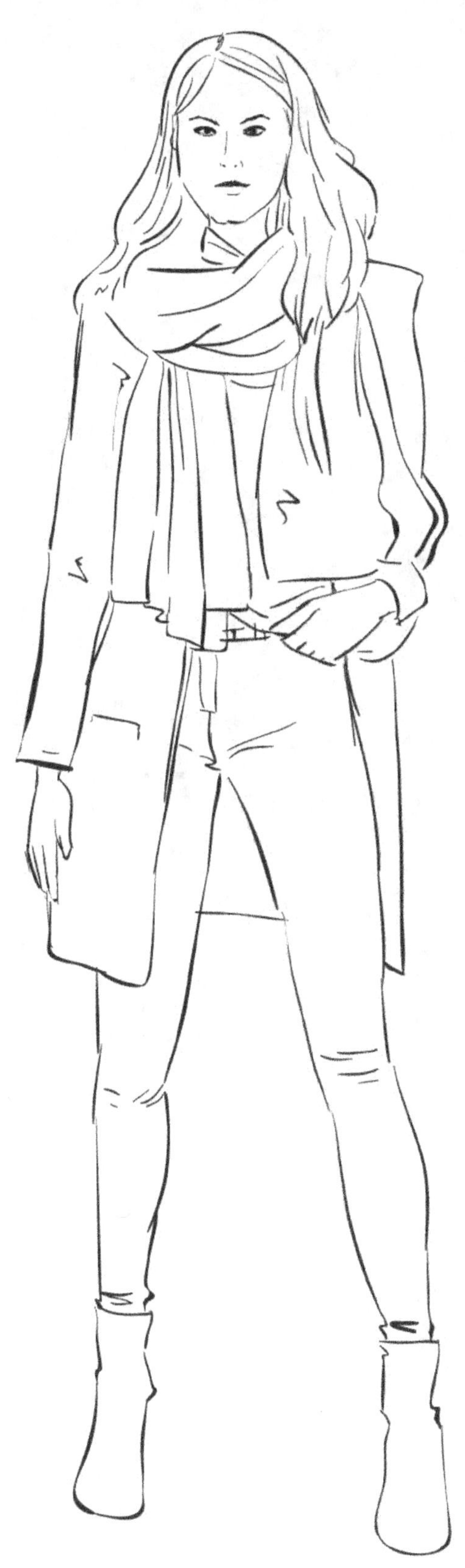

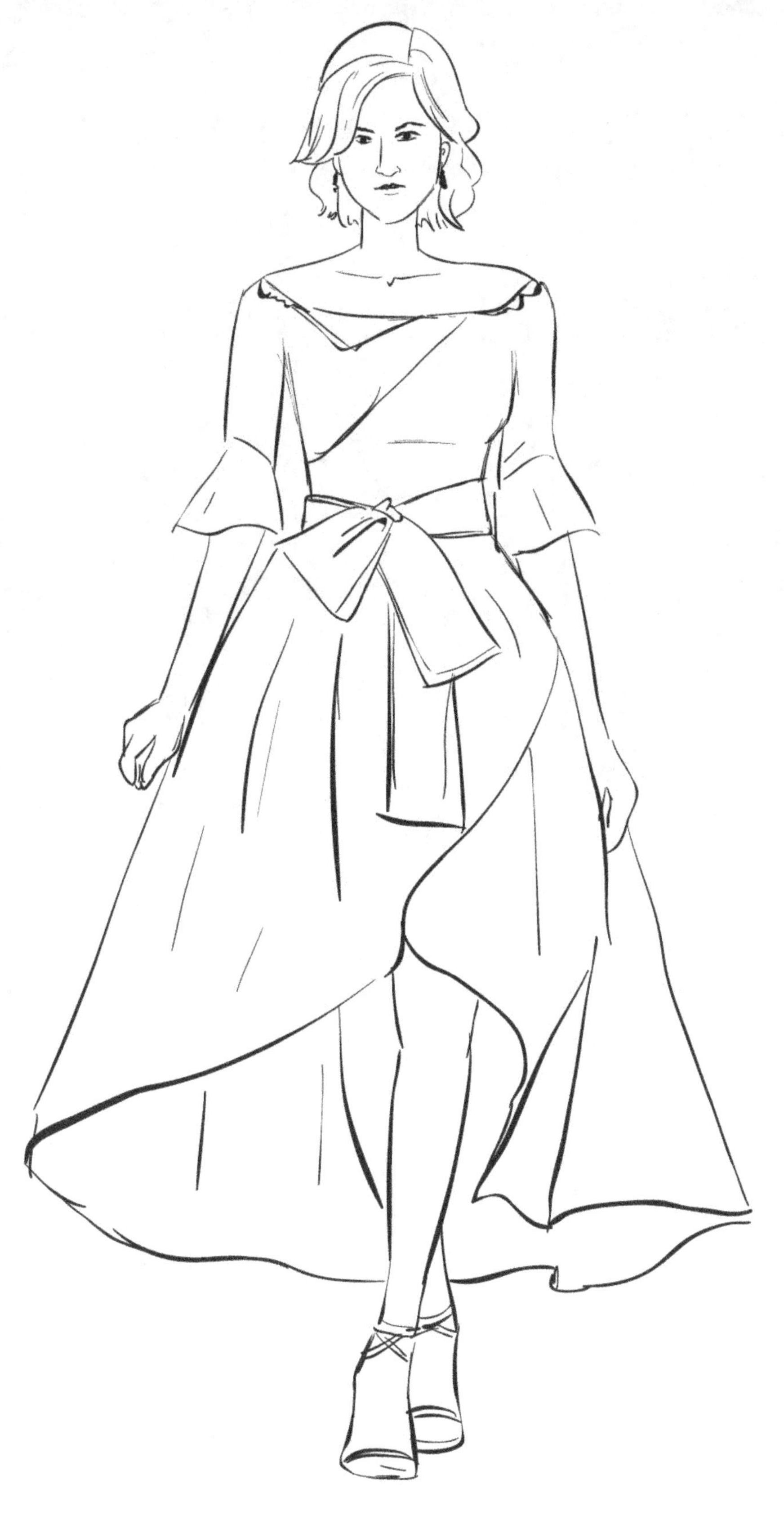

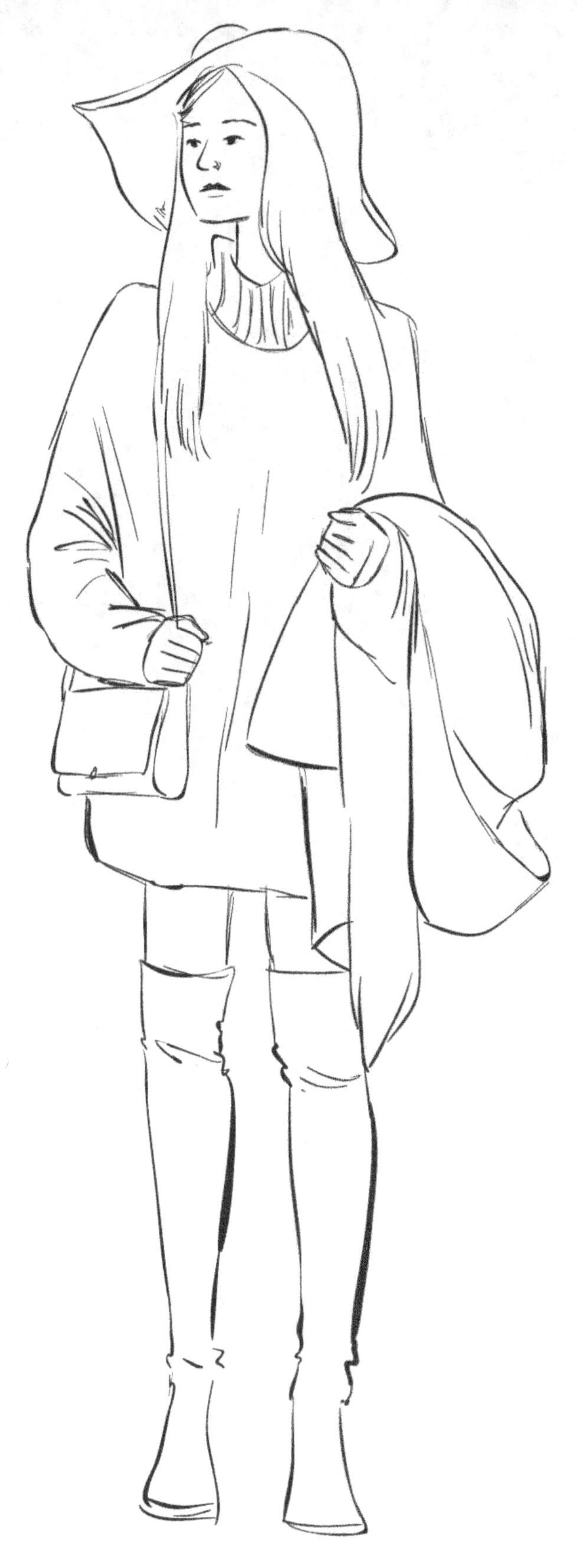

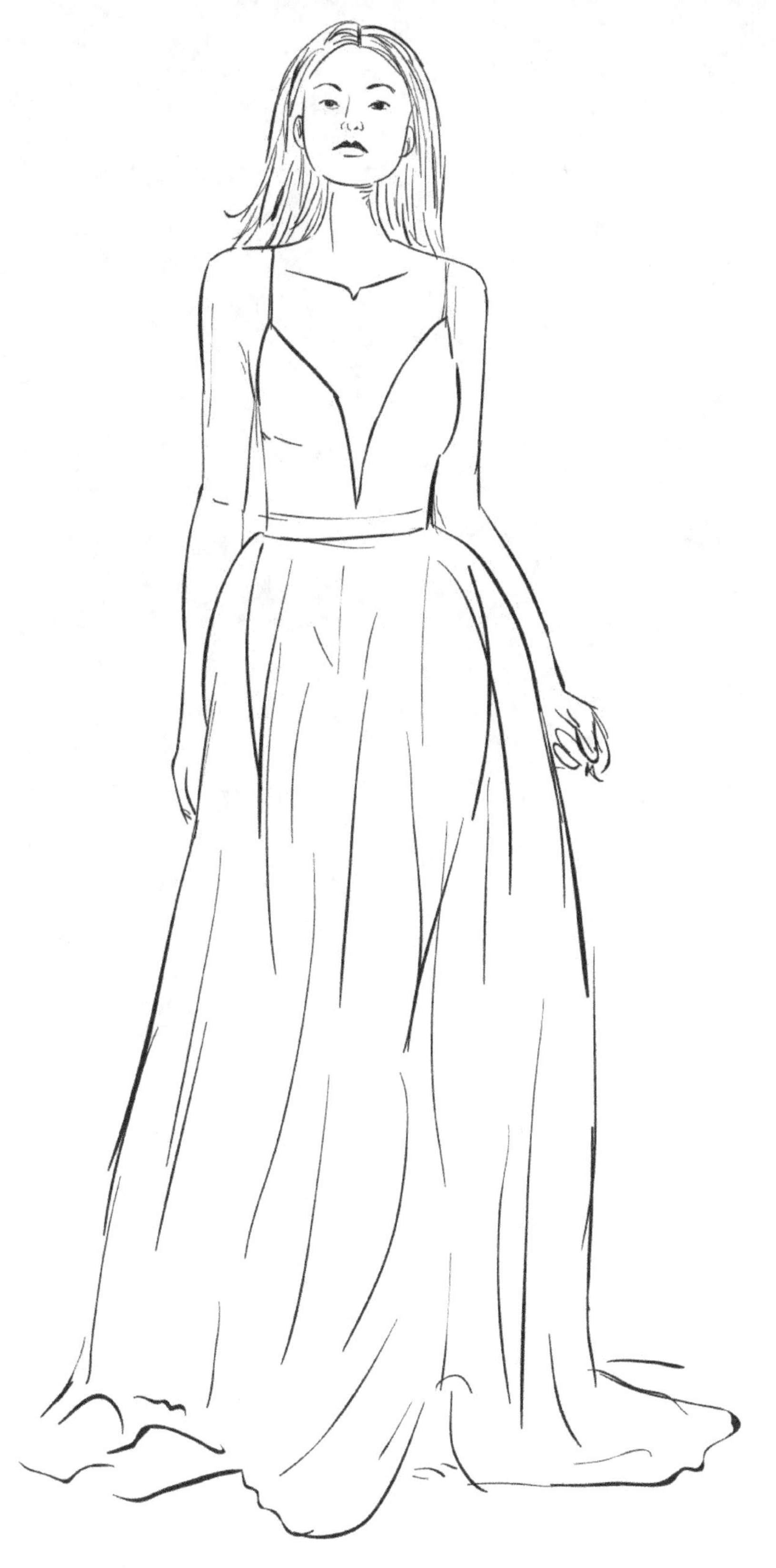

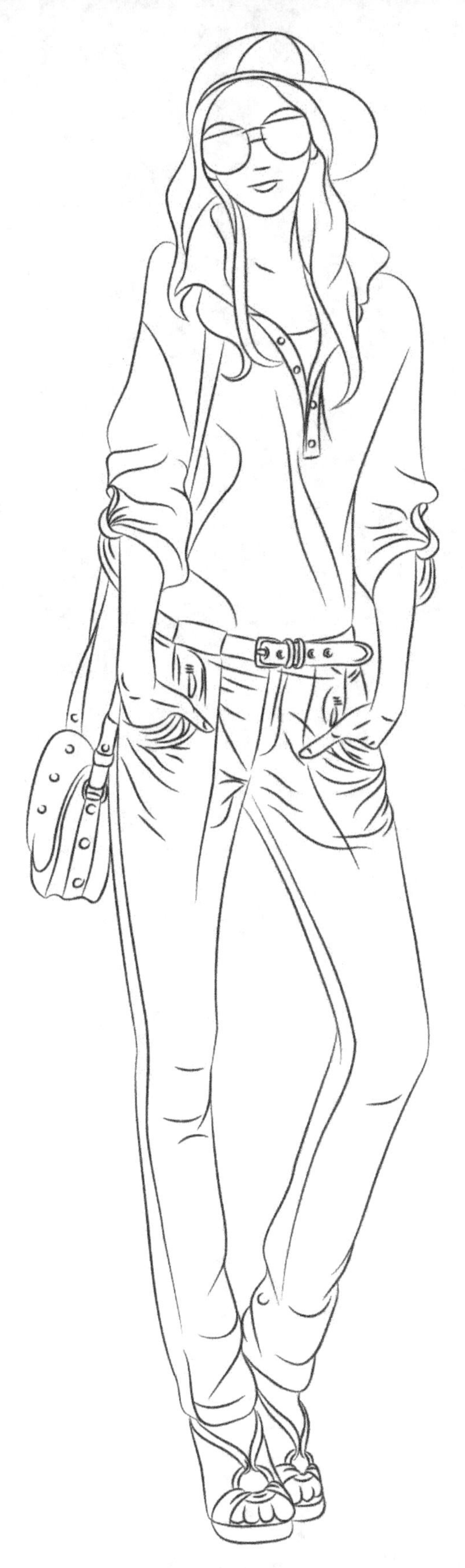

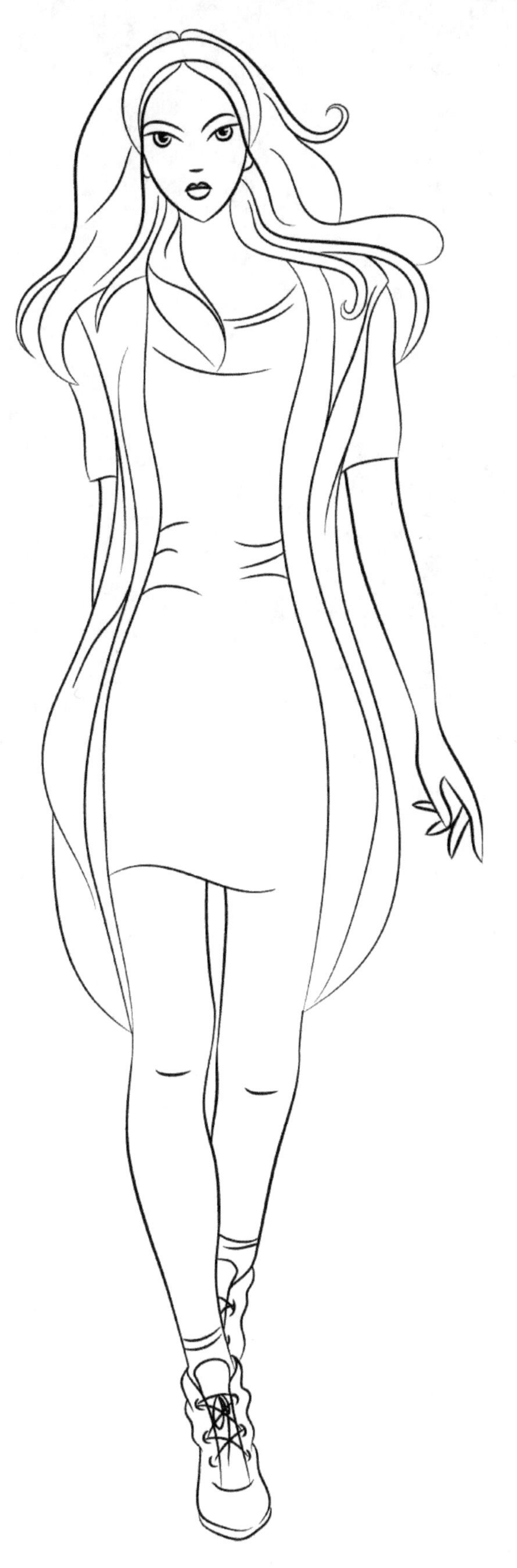

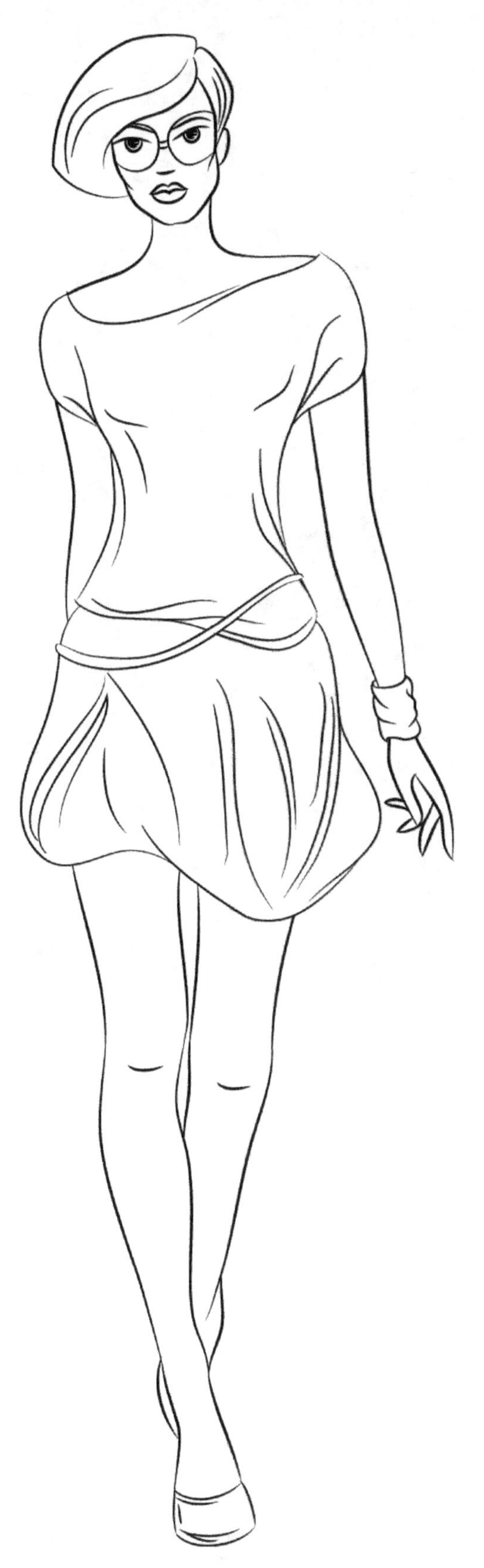

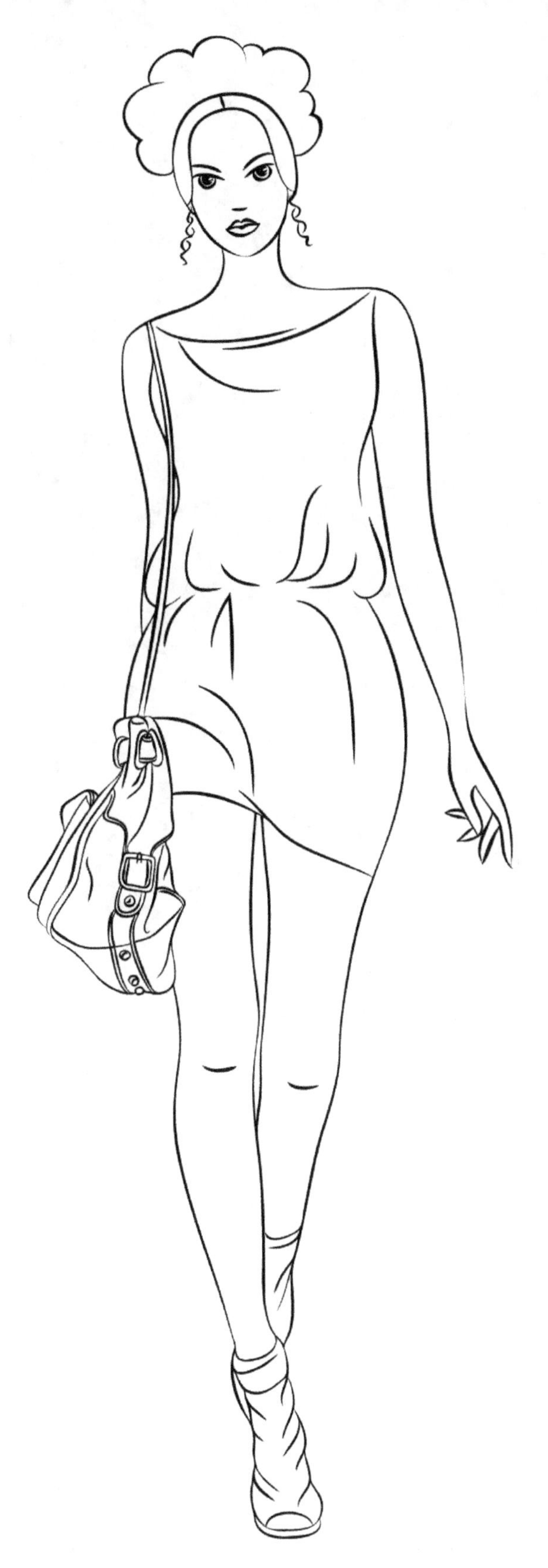

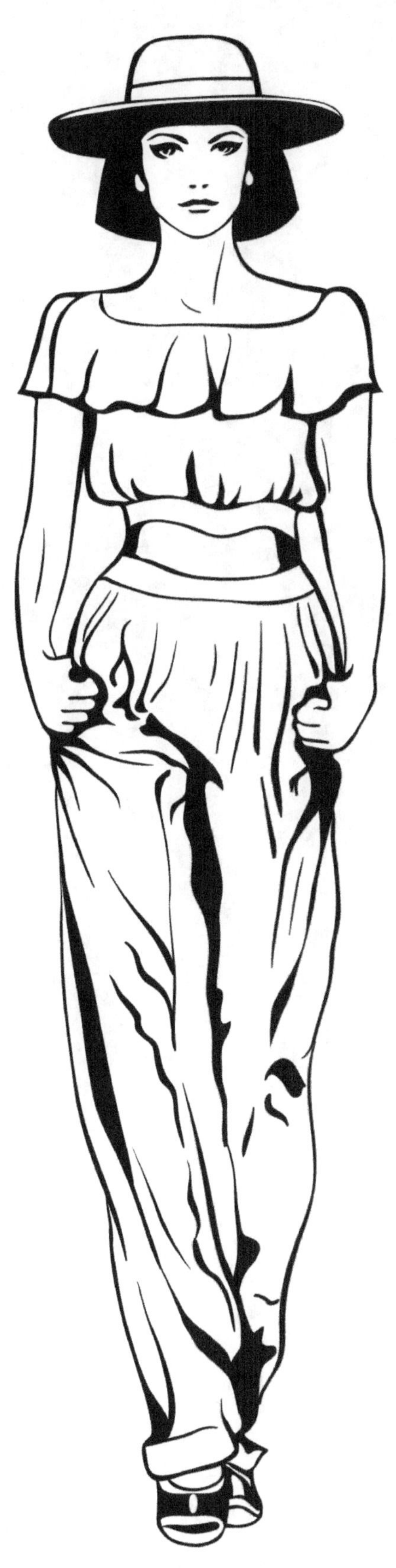

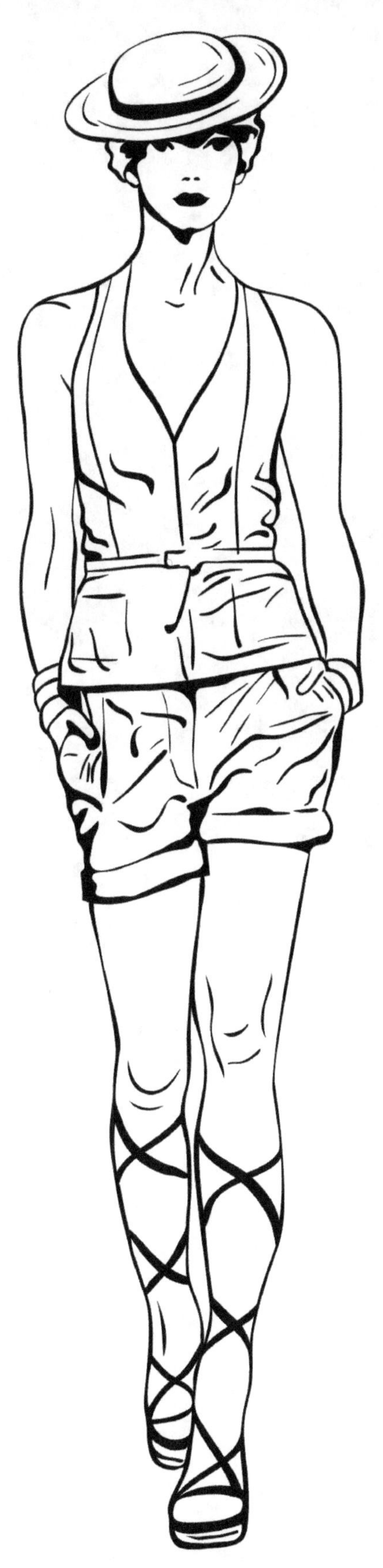

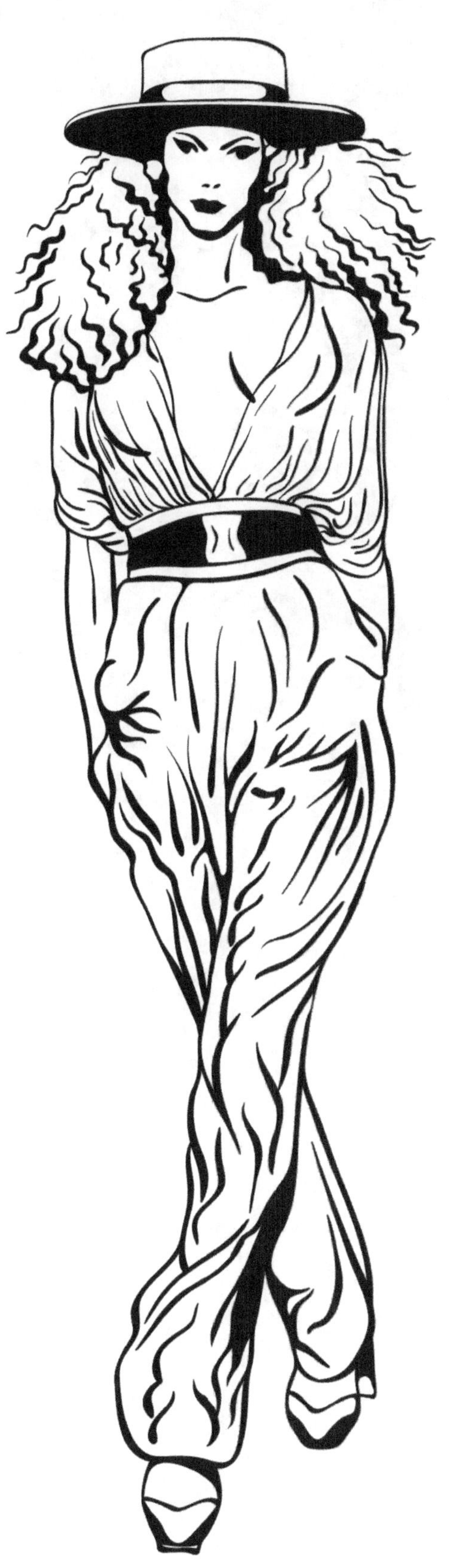

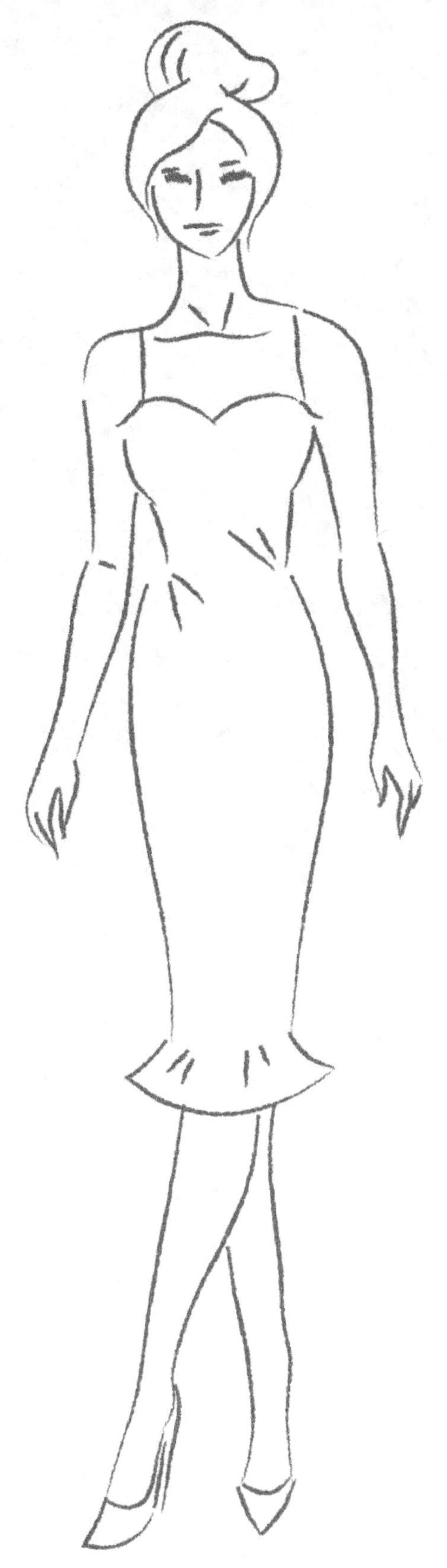

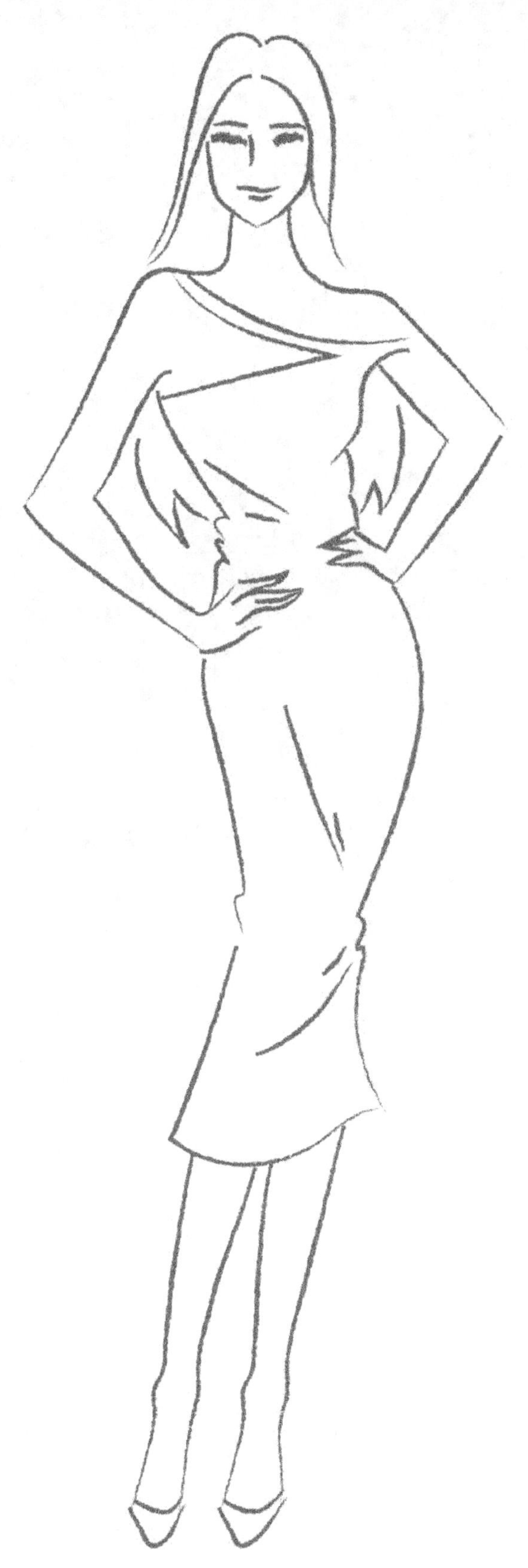

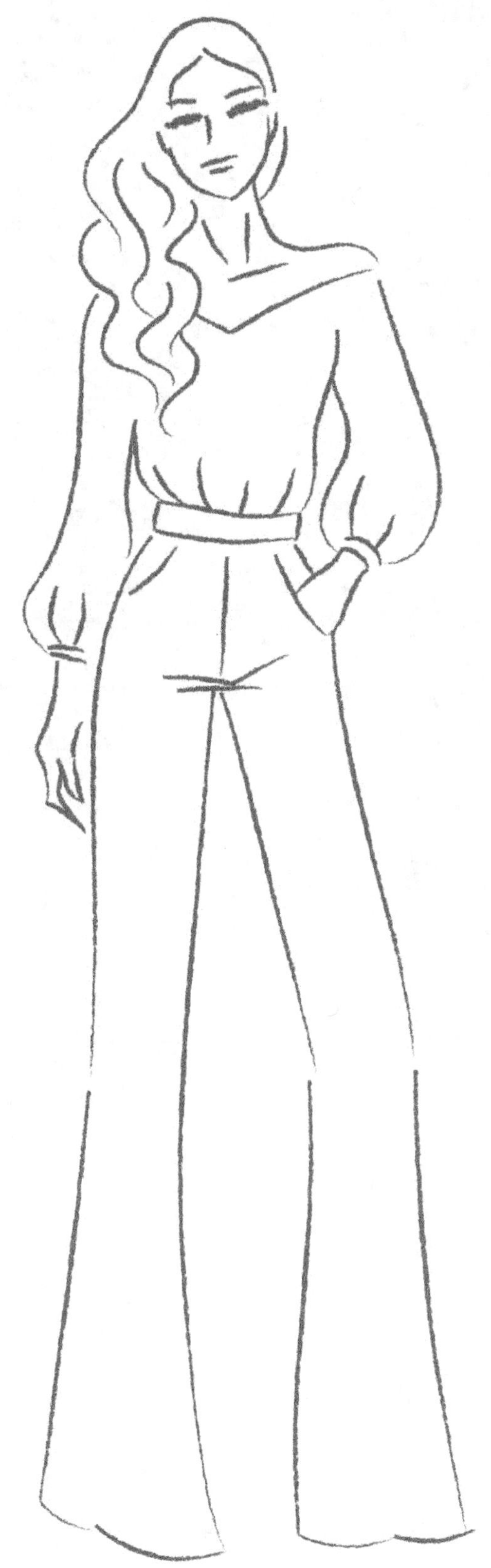

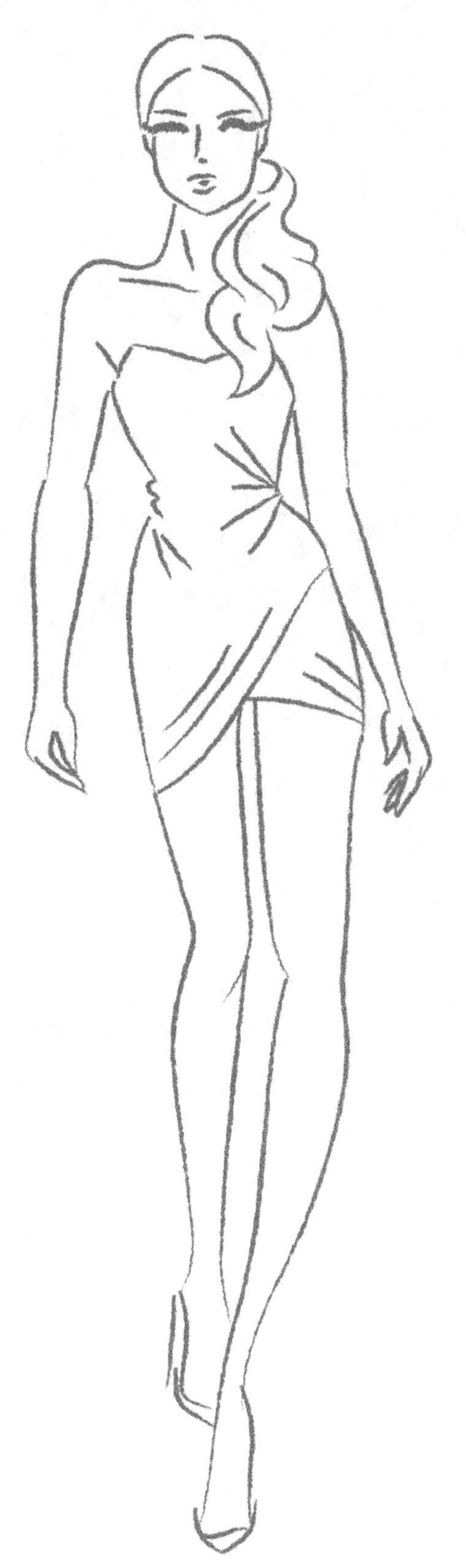

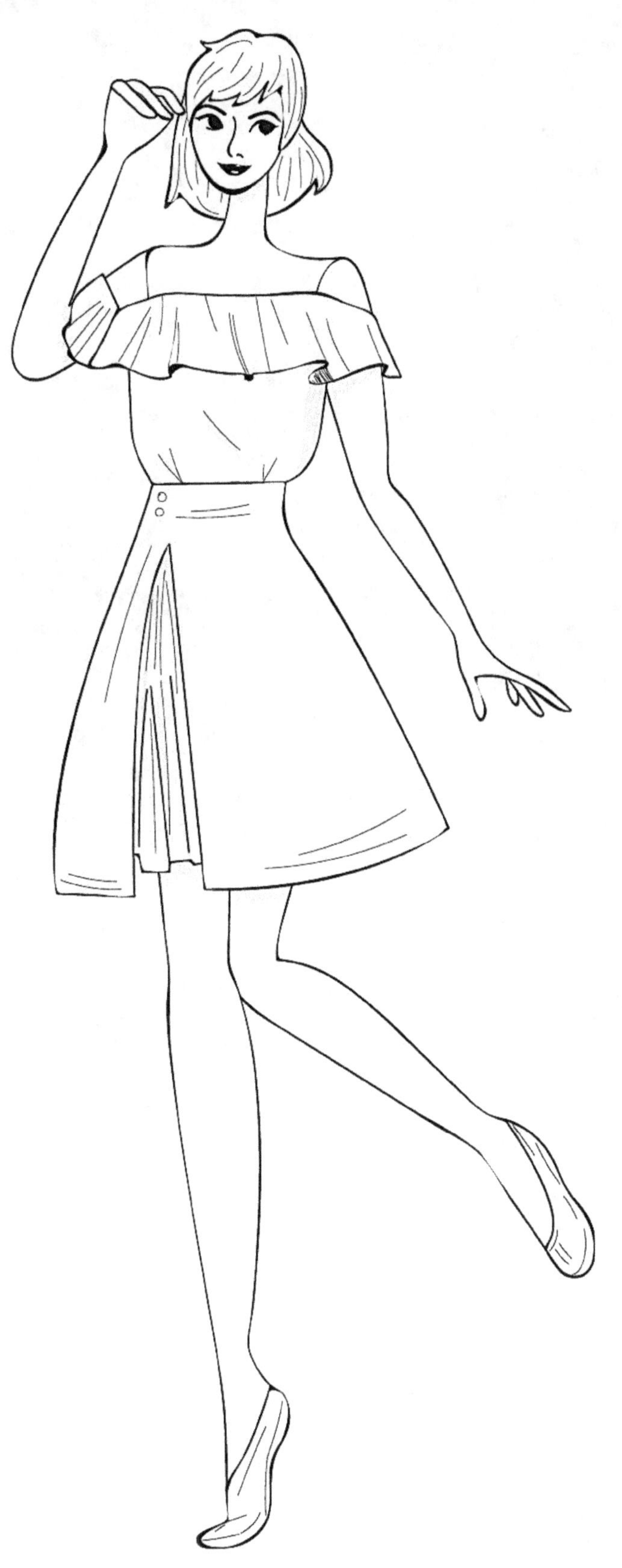

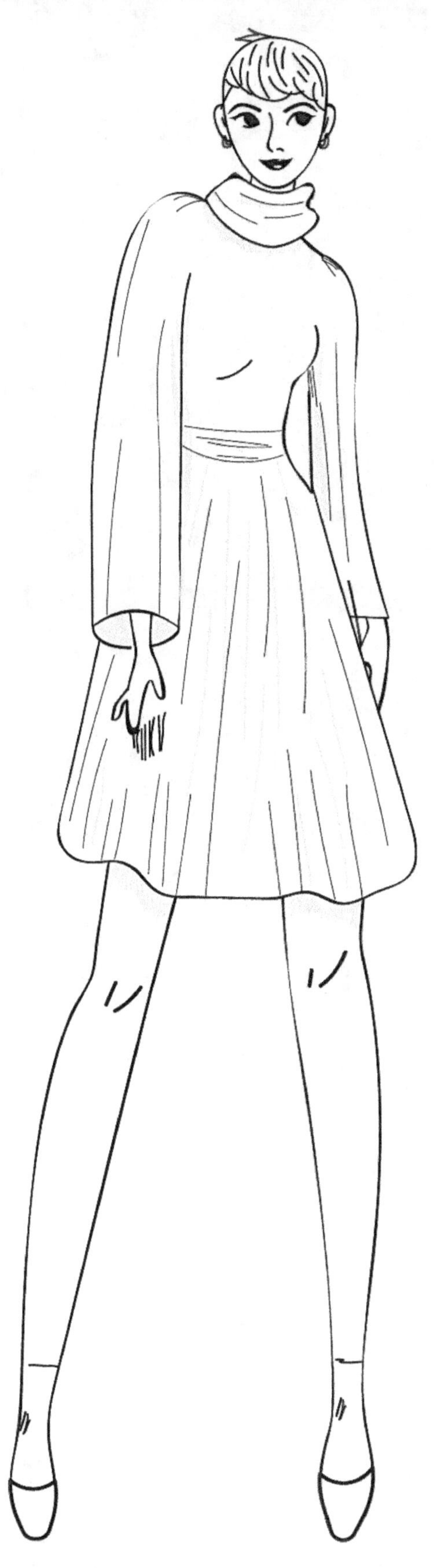

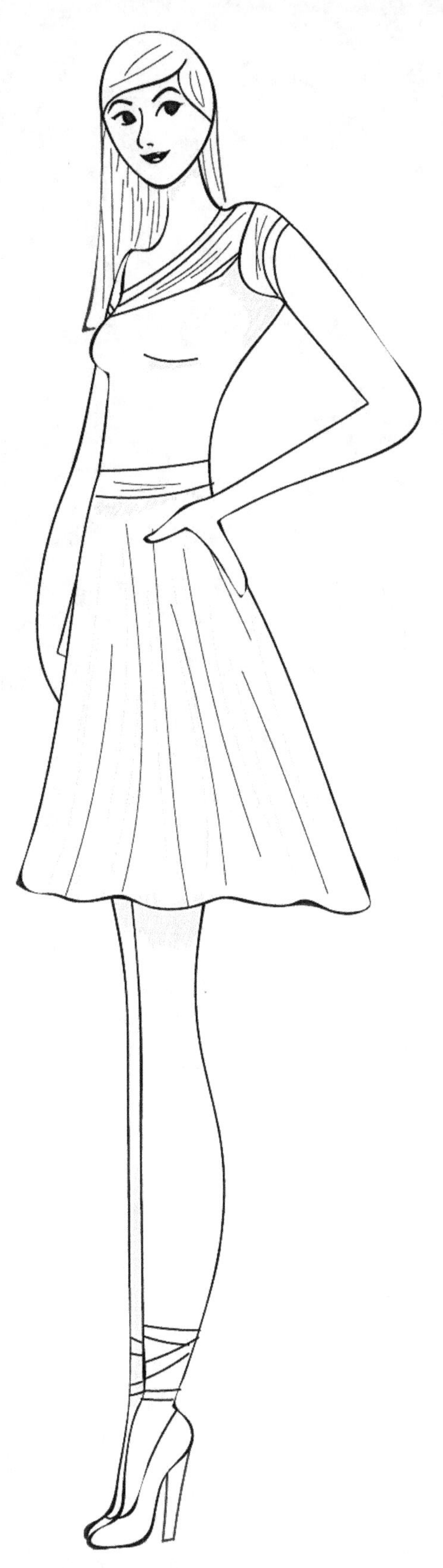

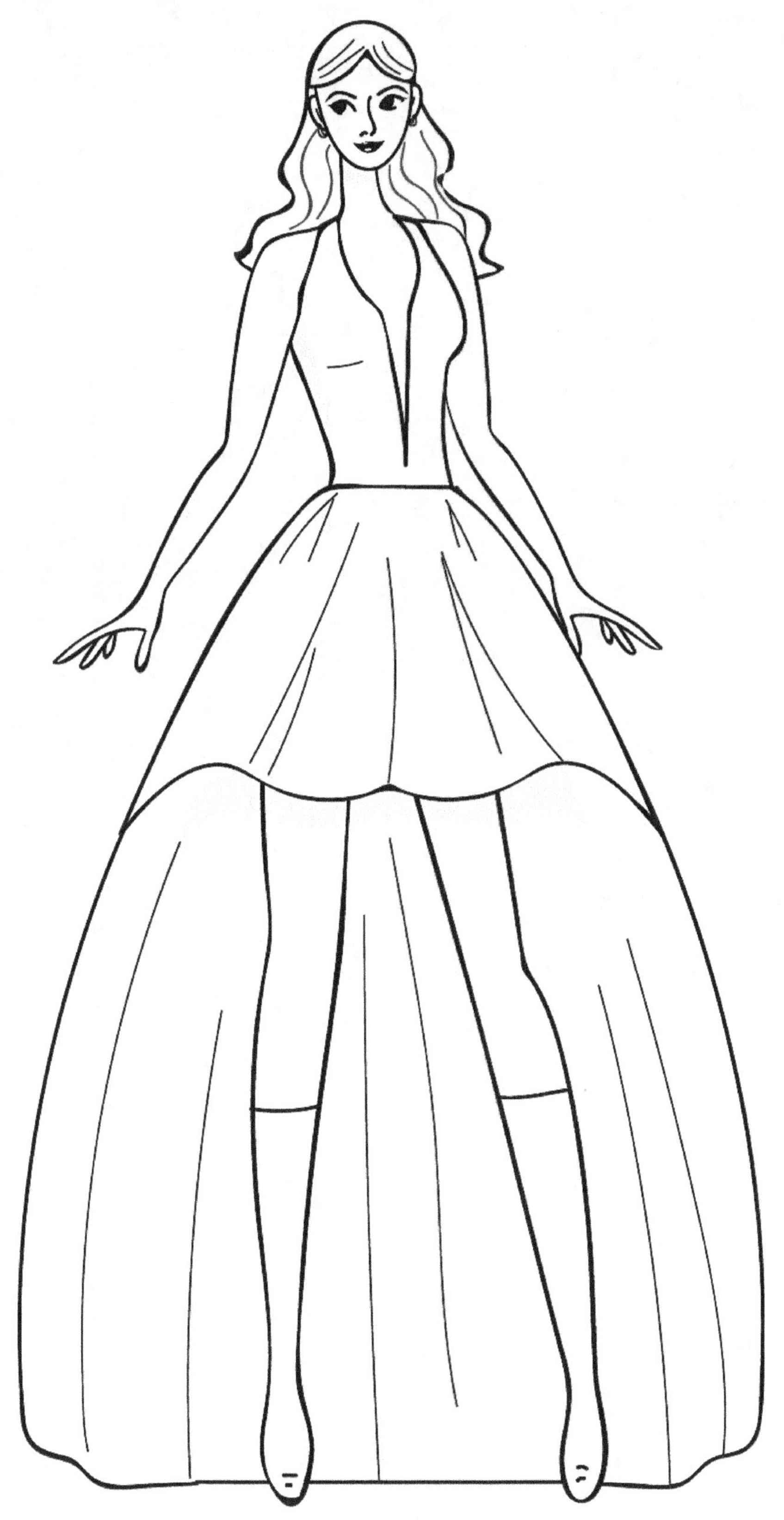

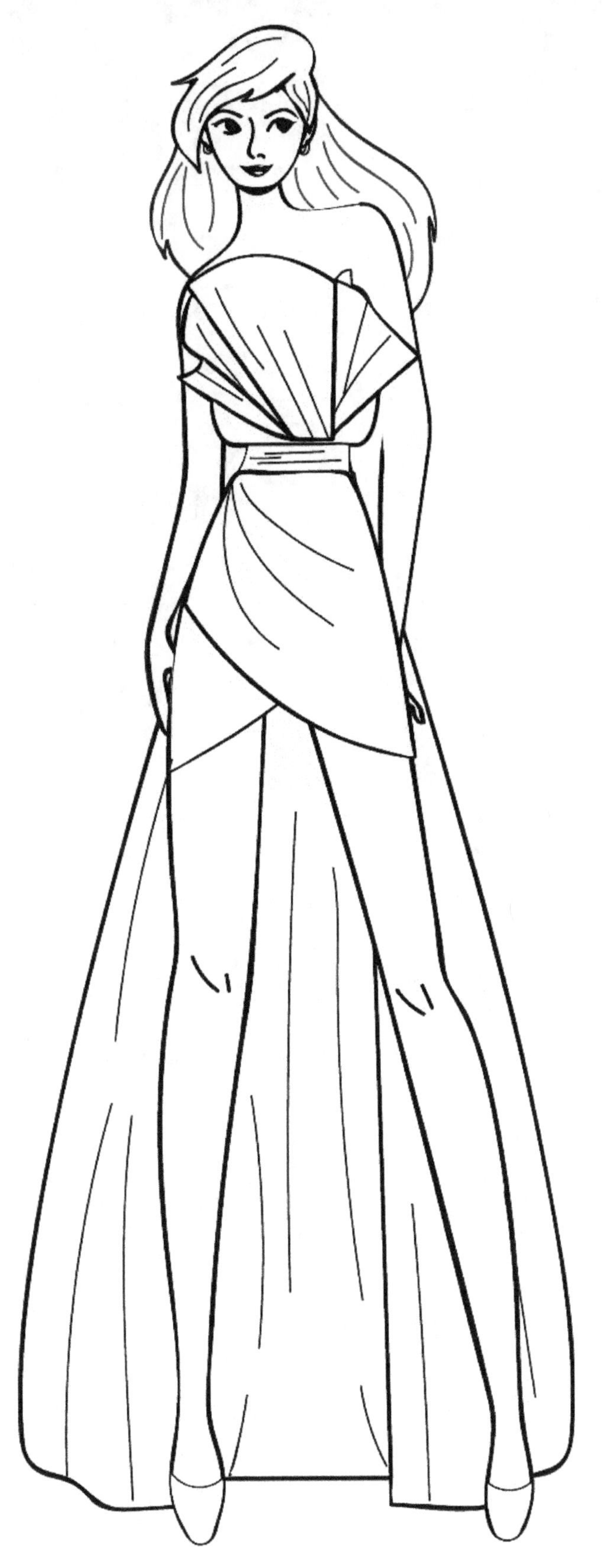

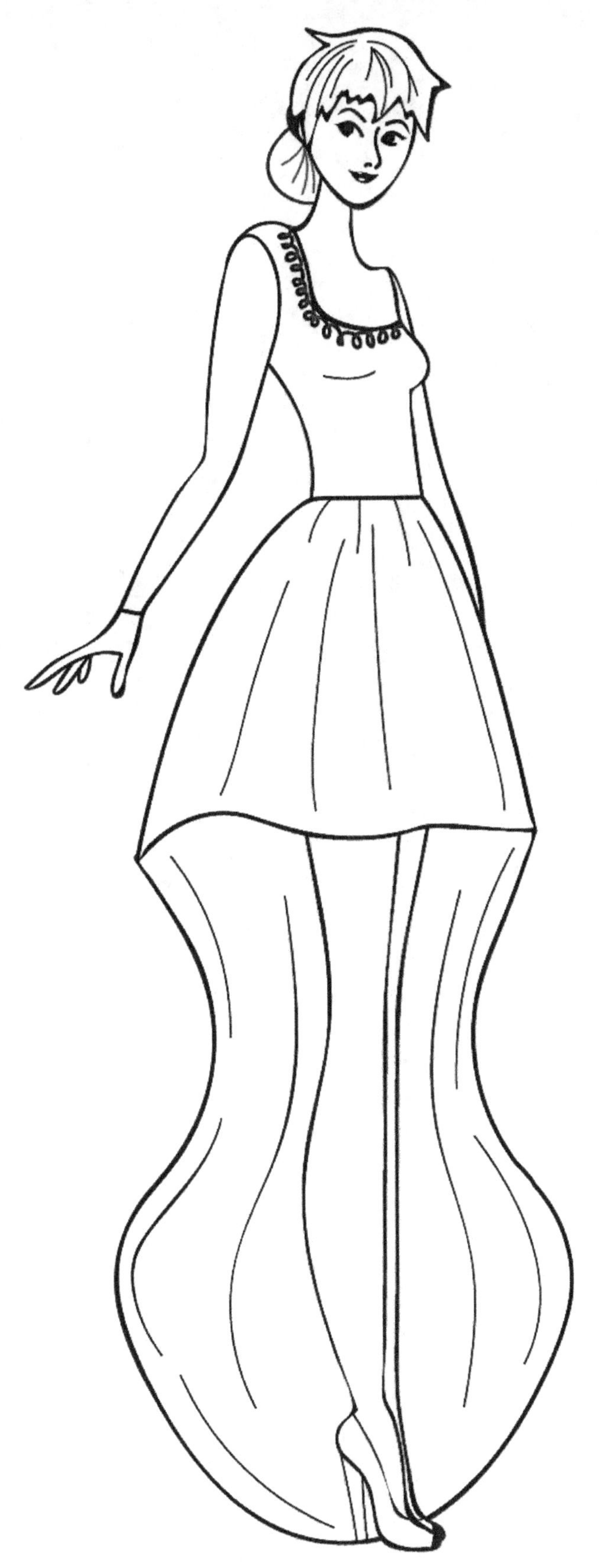

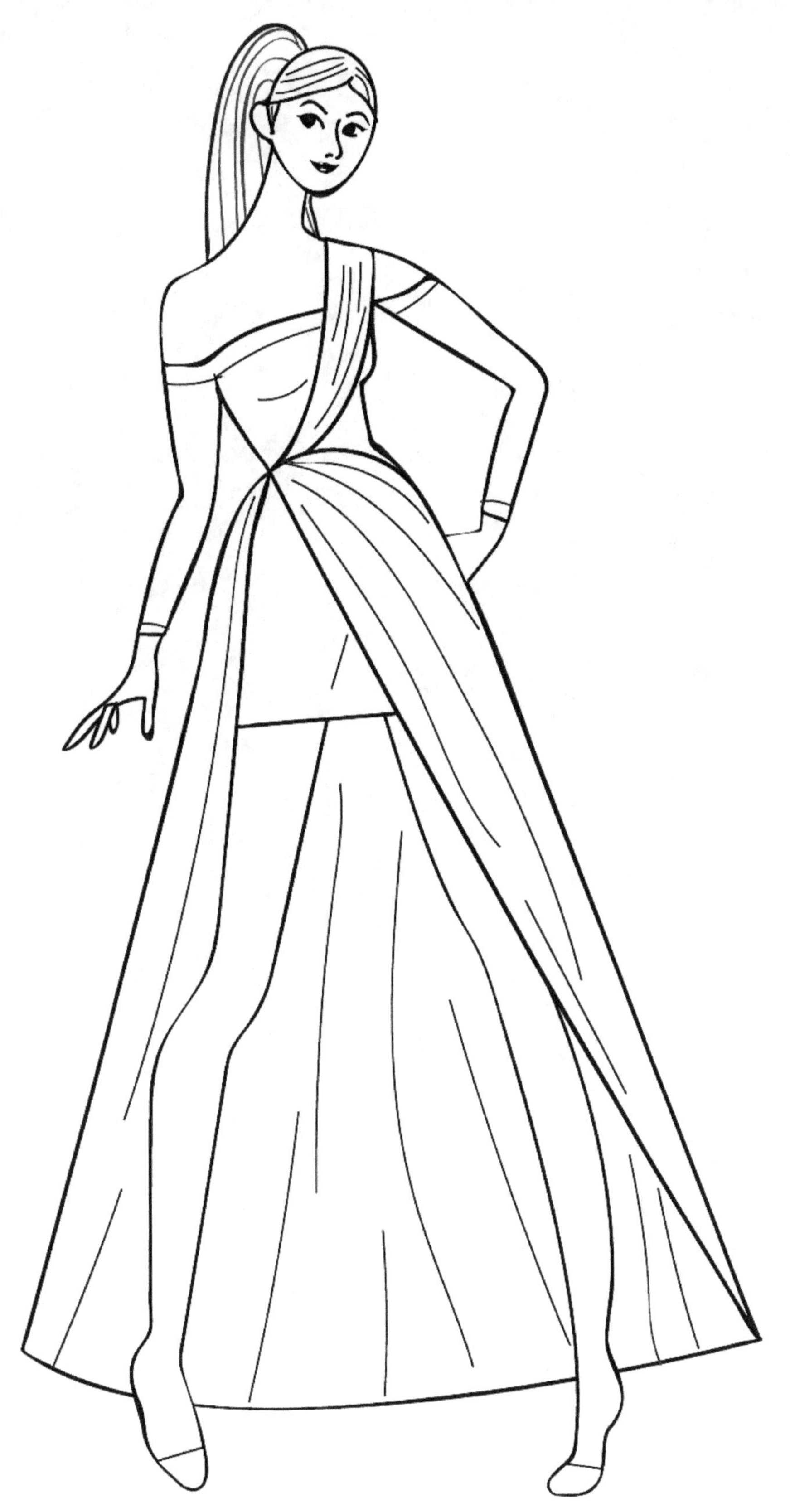

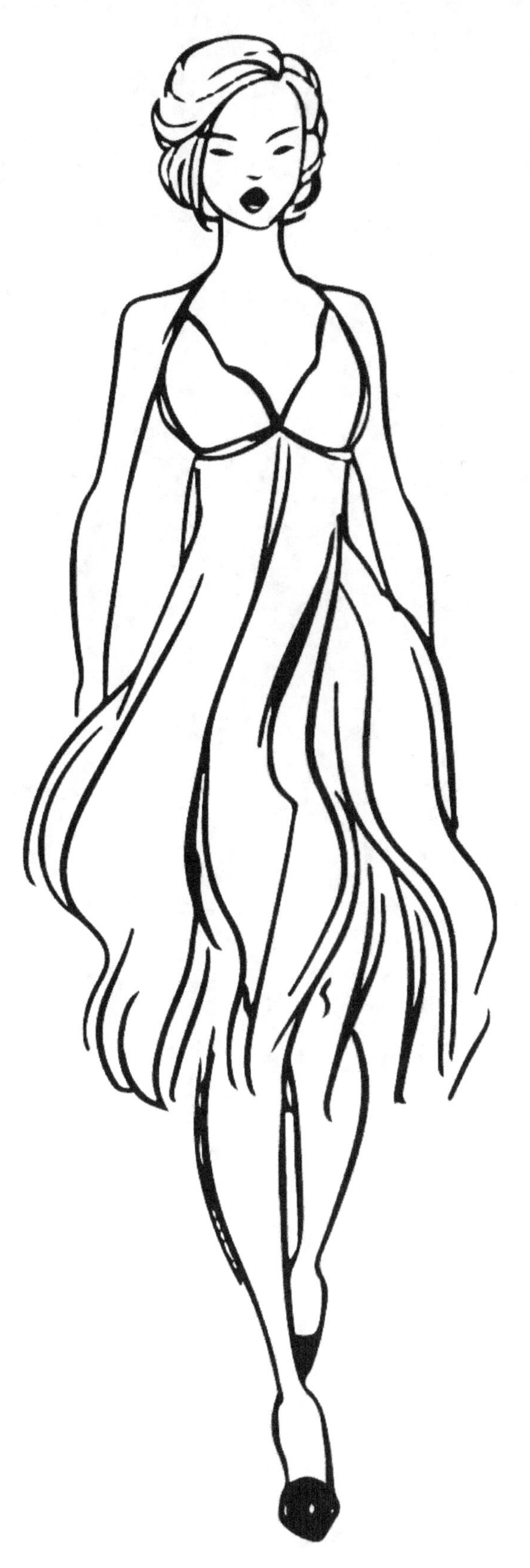

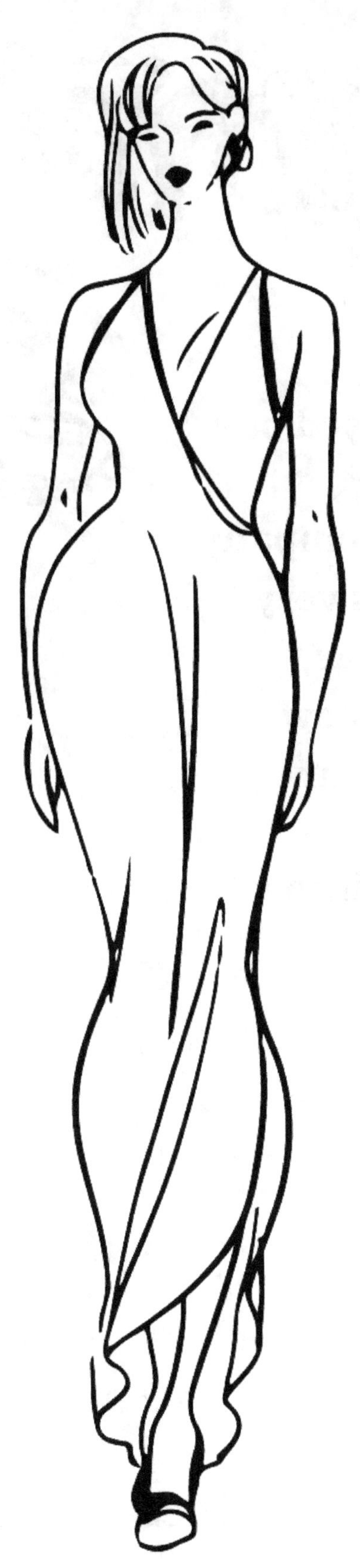

40 Outfits To Style

We hope you enjoyed our book
As a small family company, your feedback is very important to us.
Please let us know how you like our book at :
drcipcom@gmail.com

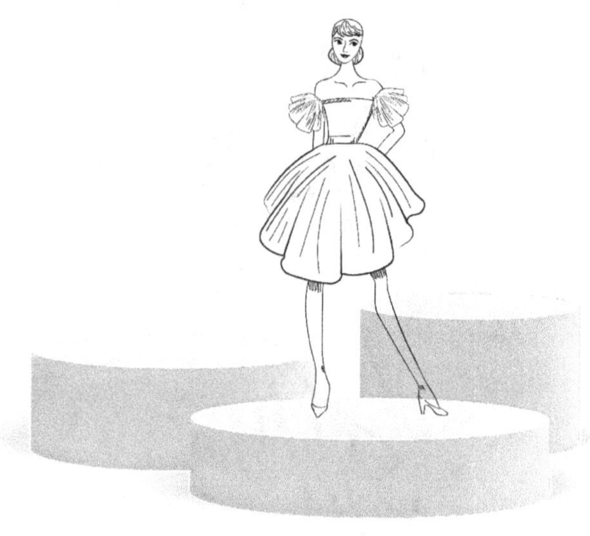